Songs in the Rough

Stephen Bishop

Songs

FROM "HEARTBREAK HOTEL"

'in

TO "HIGHER LOVE":

the

ROCK'S GREATEST SONGS

Rough

IN ROUGH-DRAFT FORM

St. Martin's Press ⚞ New York

SONGS IN THE ROUGH. Copyright © 1996 by Stephen Bishop. All rights reserved. Printed in the United States of America. No part of this book may be used or reproduced in any manner whatsoever without written permission except in the case of brief quotations embodied in critical articles or reviews. For information, address St. Martin's Press, 175 Fifth Avenue, New York, N.Y. 10010.

Library of Congress Cataloging-in-Publication Data

Bishop, Stephen.
    Songs in the rough   :   from "Heartbreak Hotel" to "Higher Love" : rock's greatest songs in rough-draft form / Stephen Bishop.
        p.   cm.
    ISBN 0-312-14048-7
    1. Rock music—History and criticism. 2. Rock music—Manuscripts—Facsimiles. 3. Rock musicians—Interviews. I. Title.
ML3534.B57 1996
782.42166'0262—dc20   95-45128
                                                      CIP
                                                      MN

First edition: June 1996

10 9 8 7 6 5 4 3 2 1

I dedicate this book to my brother, Denny,

who bought me my first guitar.

Acknowledgments

Acknowledgments

This book could not have been done without the help of these people: Barbara Cane; Barbara Dale; BMI; Jeff Leve; Scott Welch; Geanie Zelig-Galinson; Fred Goldring; Mark Jaffe; NAS; Pam Janney and Steve Routhier, Hard Rock Cafe East; Warick Stone, Hard Rock Cafe West; Linda Ronstadt; Philip Graham; Gloria Boyce; Steve Schachlin; Dan Kilpatrick; Micky Dolenz; Ron Wilson; Jay Morganstern; Kim Wilkerson; Erin Hogan; Sammy Cahn; Shirley Westover; John Jarvis; Jim Wilson; Arthur Hamilton; Chris Skinker, Country Music Hall of Fame; Dick Ashby; Michael Bruce; Brian Doyle; Henry Diltz; Jim Henke; Mark Linett; Michael Ochs; Peter Stiglin; Dave Olson; Suzy Vaughan; Ron McGowan; Mae Boren Axton; Annette Flowers; Jim David; Will Jennings; Linda Lou Bouch; Justin Hayward; Diane Warren; Brendan Okrent; Kathy Gates, Butterfield & Butterfield; Jono, Symphony Cafe; Del Bryant; Phil Collins; Don Williams; Michael Eames; David Leaf; Jane Arginteanu; Ingrid Croce; Mike McCartney; Andy Goldmark; Angie Dickinson; Sharyn Felder; Tracey Ross; Pattie Dahlstrom; Shirli Dixon; Marie Dixon; Lynn Goldsmith; David Sanjek; Kathy Carey; Paul Meisner; Jeff Jones; Mrs. Robin Gibb.

Special Thanks

Special thanks: Susan Morris; Linda Ronstadt; Frances Preston; Kathy Carey; Paige Sober; Mac Davis; Doreen Ringer; Geoffrey Blumenauer; Shelley Wiseman, Jackson Browne; Marc Cohn; Perry Cooper; Michael Fairchild; Rebecca Bishop; Bennett Freed; Frank Fuchs; Janis Ian; Steve Kipner; Linda Perry; Bill Siddons; Jeff Silbar; Cathy Kerr, Randy Newman; Linda Lou Bouch; Justin Hayward; Jack Keller; Diane Warren; Mason Williams; Marie Dixon; Shirli Dixon; Lynn Goldsmith; Jon Landau; Marcus Peterzell; Jeff Rosen; Rick Riccobono; Cal Morgan; Pei Loi Koay; Twisne Fan; Lisa Vecchione; Larry Klein; Harold Bronson.

Personal Assistants: Emily Pruitt; Lisa Latham; Lanie Handleman; Mikki Lesowitz.

Contents

Preface
xiii

PART ONE: IN THE BEGINNING
xvi

You Are My Sunshine • This Land Is Your Land • Save the Last Dance for Me • Heartbreak Hotel • Bye Bye Love • Wake Up Little Susie • Hello Mary Lou, Goodbye Heart • Runaway • My Special Angel • Monster Mash • Meet the Flintstones • Mama Said • I'm On My Way

PART TWO: SUNSHINE DAYS
26

Good Day Sunshine • Penny Lane • Lovely Rita • Lucy in the Sky with Diamonds • Sgt. Pepper's Lonely Hearts Club Band • Sunshine Superman • Ferry Cross the Mersey • This Diamond Ring • Psychotic Reaction • This Old Heart of Mine • Surf's Up • Daydream Believer • Somebody to Love • Rocky Top • I Was Made to Love Her • Chicago • Crosstown Traffic • Purple Haze • Never My Love • Sugar Magnolia • God • Pledging My Time

PART THREE: PEACEFUL FEELINGS
58

I Think I Love You • Raindrops Keep Fallin' on My Head • We've Only Just Begun • Jammin' • Levon • You Don't Mess Around with Jim • Peaceful Easy Feeling • Best of My Love • Heartache Tonight • She's Gone • Ooh Las Vegas • The Way We Were • Only Women Bleed • No More Mr. Nice Guy • Rhiannon • Rock and Roll All Nite • Mamas Don't Let Your Babies Grow Up to Be Cowboys • Sometimes at Night • Tenth Avenue Freeze Out • Stayin' Alive • On and On

PART FOUR: THE MTV YEARS
98

Separate Lives • Lives in the Balance • Fame • Promises in the Dark • My Bologna • We Got the Beat • Invisible Touch • Sussudio • One More Night • Higher Love • Baby Grand • Soul Provider • I Wanna Dance with Somebody • From a Distance • Copperline • Rhythm Nation • I Touch Myself • Yvette in English • Study War No More

Song Credits
138

Preface

At the age of five, I discovered a record called "The Legend of Davy Crockett." I went around singing the chorus over and over again until everyone around me became quite ill. I had no idea who wrote it or why; it was just there, and I dug it. From that point on, I started becoming aware of this thing called *music*. All of a sudden, I started to notice songs coming at me from all over the place—the radio, the television, even at church. I used to stand in Sunday school and wait for my favorite hymn to come up: page 234, the sixth-century inspirational "Onward Christian Soldiers." I'd give it everything I had, feeling the melody go through me, taking me up to the rafters. It was the only song I liked to sing in church. Within a year, I was singing "Three Coins in a Fountain" full-throttle as I swept our front-porch steps.

At the age of ten I had an experience that would have a very strong effect on my life. I'd been waiting for my dad to take me to the annual Elks' Christmas party. There was always a giant Christmas tree with lots of toys underneath it for all the little Elk children. My parents had recently divorced, and my relationship with my dad was still a little awkward. I waited and waited for him to show, and as time went by I started to worry that we'd miss the party. Finally, his white Chevrolet pulled up, and we sped off. As we got to the Elks' Lodge I dashed into the big hall, only to discover the old Elk guys tearing everything down. The Christmas party was over. The hall was empty. I could hear the faint sounds of creepy kids laughing in the parking lot. At the end of the big hall stood a giant Christmas tree, without a single present under it.

My dad, in his best Ward Cleaver voice, said, "Maybe there's a present stuck somewhere under the tree, son." I ran up there and searched and searched, but there was nothing left. I was starting to lose it. We were about to leave when my dad noticed something sticking out among the branches. It was a tiny present, with a little tear on the side of the wrapping. I held it in my hands as we walked out to the car. It didn't look like much, and I was doing your basic ten-year-old sulking thing when he said, "Son, why don't you open it? They say good things come in small—"

"Yeah, right, I've heard that before. . . . Well, okay . . . " I unwrapped it, and to my genuine surprise it was a shiny yellow two-transistor pocket radio. My dad was off the hook—and seemed almost as pleased as I was.

Having your own radio was a wonderful thing for a ten-year-old in 1961. We were a low-income family, living off the freeway near the mountains in San Diego. There weren't any kids to hang around with, so that little radio became my best friend. I'd play it in the treehouse my brother Denny built for me; the radio only got two stations, but the music that came out of it took me to another place—to the land of Top Forty. I had it all up there, songs from all over the world, blasting out of my little two-transistor while my mom tried to find me for dinner.

All those songs were written by human beings whose ideas and bits and pieces of melody and lyric were turned into modern treasures. And—as I'd learn much later, when I started to write songs—nearly every time a song was written, there was a rough draft that went along with it.

A rough draft is a musical blueprint of what happens in the embryonic stages of a new song, a map of its progress from idea into anthem. A rough draft, more often than not, contains the cross-outs, line changes, jottings-down, alternate titles, doodles, and marginalia that can turn a little jolt of inspiration and a few minutes of effort into royalty checks that last a lifetime. Even the two best-known songs of all time started out a little different from the way they ended up: Before the rough draft became a final draft, the Hill sisters' "Happy Birthday to You" was "Good Morning to You," and Paul McCartney's "Yesterday" went under the working title "Scrambled Eggs."

A scribbled idea on a napkin or on a torn piece of paper, a few lines on a restaurant bill, even lyric ideas written on a first-class boarding pass—these are just a few of the many items I've encountered in my three years of putting this book together. I discovered that some of the most beloved songs of the past thirty years had been jotted down at odd moments, in pencil, on the back of what would otherwise qualify as trash. Unfortunately, for every rough draft that survived, countless others made it only as far as the trash bin. One of the first songwriters I spoke to was the brilliant Cynthia Weil, who with Barry Mann wrote hits from "You've Lost that Lovin' Feeling" to "Just Once." "No, we never kept anything," she told me. "I could hardly wait to throw things away." Maybe after she sees this book she'll start saving those scraps of paper.

I wound up meeting all kinds of wonderful people in the process of working on this book, songwriters I'd always admired and who turned out to be some of the most fascinating people I've ever met: Felice Bryant, who with her husband Boudleaux wrote some of the most memorable songs of the fifties, including: "Wake Up Little Susie," "Bye Bye Love," "(All I Have to Do Is) Dream." Sammy Cahn, who helped me find the rough draft of "Heartbreak Hotel" in the basement of the Symphony Cafe in New York. Bobby Hart, the late Tommy Boyce, and other songwriters who wished they'd kept what they'd thrown away. I had to dig way down at times to get up the courage to call some of these writers; I've never been the kind of guy who enjoys hounding people, but I learned how: "Have you found it yet?" "Where did you keep your old songbooks?" "Did your daughter come over yet to help you look for it in the garage?"

I hit many dead ends along the way, and experienced many disappointments. I was disheartened to find that none of the roughs from Motown's Holland-Dozier-Holland stable can be found. I had a tough time finding a lot of old R&B or blues songs. Once, at the end of a rough day of searching, while leaving a message for a songwriter, I sang the melody of "Since I Fell for You" into his answering machine instead of "Since I Don't Have You"; I haven't heard from him since. I was just leaving a hotel room in New York when the phone rang: "Hello, Stephen, it's Bob Wells." At first I couldn't place the name, until I remembered that he'd written a little song with Mel Torme—"The Christmas Song" ("Chestnuts roasting on an open fire . . ."). I was elated . . . until he told me that the rough draft would remain in its frame in his dining room. I tracked down the writer of "Blue Velvet," and his wife nicely told me he'd get to it once he felt a little better. I called and left messages for the next few months; I gave up one day after sadly reading his obituary in the newspaper.

But, with the help of good friends in the business and the many songwriters I know personally, I started to have some success. The name of the book, *Songs in the Rough,* was suggested by a songwriter friend of mine, Jeff Jones. Gene Pitney's mom, I learned, had saved all her son's rough drafts—rescuing them from the trash basket after he threw them away. It's almost unbelievable that Boris Pickett's just-barely legible "Monster Mash" *wasn't* thrown away at some point, but it miraculously survived. Many of the pieces in this book were saved by the sons, daughters, wives, and widows of the writers; others were gifts to friends or old girlfriends. And some writers were attached enough to their own history to hold onto their early roughs. They're all showcased now as song history.

To me, it's fascinating to examine the differences between these seventy-odd rough drafts—taken from every period in the rock era, from every kind of songwriter, at every stage in the songwriting process. Some of the roughs come from late in the drafting process and as a result look like neatly drawn homework assignments: Weird Al Yankovic's "My Bologna"—his first hit—for example, has only a few minor changes.

But many of the other songs here reveal all kinds of unexpected things about the writers and the songwriting process. Clearly inspired by the moment, Doc Pomus scribbled what became the title of "Save the Last Dance for Me" on his own wedding invitation. Robin Gibb wrote some crucial lyric lines of the Bee Gees' "Stayin' Alive" on a British Airways ticket while he was bound for Miami. "You Don't Mess Around with Jim," "Peaceful Easy Feeling," and "I Think I Love You" got started on restaurant bills, rent tabulations, record sleeves; Paul Williams even jotted down the idea for "We've Only Just Begun" on the proverbial back of the envelope. The original sheet for "Fame" reveals a terrific collaboration, with the two songwriters adding to and improving upon the original typed lyrics. And most of the songs here, from "Heartbreak Hotel" to "I Touch Myself," reveal that, rather than being starved for inspiration, many of rock's greatest songwriters leave as much on the cutting-room floor as they put into the songs themselves. For me, that's the fun of looking at these rough drafts: watching the process of trial and error that can lead a songwriter to write a song that becomes a part of our lives—a part of musical history.

But, to be honest, I can't claim that my getting started on *Songs in the Rough* was entirely a matter of scholarly drive. This project would never have begun without a bizarre incident back in the spring of 1992.

Some friends were having a party, and I'd volunteered to bring over some cheese. As I put the rounds of Brie in the trunk of my car, something suddenly snapped in my right wrist as I was stowing the cheese in the trunk. I started to get that "uh-oh" kind of feeling—I could barely move my fingers. I'd been playing a lot of tennis that week, but I blamed the cheese. I'd always had problems with dairy, but hey. . . .

After going to several doctors, I discovered that I'd torn a major ligament. I had an operation, they put pins in my wrist, and I stayed in an elbow-length cast for two months. What really freaked me out, though, was that I wasn't able to play guitar that whole time. No guitar! I was not thrilled; the thought of not playing seemed catastrophic—I'd go nuts without something to do. So one day I just decided it must be fate: Maybe I should finally get this book idea going. So I positioned myself in bed with the phone, music chartbooks by my side, and started calling everybody I knew who could help me with this near-impossible task—to find the little acorns from which the tall oak trees would grow.

I've had a lot of schemes and ideas in the past that have just faded away, but I thought this was something I might actually be able to pull off. I had no idea how difficult it would be, how all of my friends would be driven crazy with my incessant obsession: the Ultimate Rough Draft. And I'm still looking. . . .

—Stephen Bishop

In the Beginning

Governor Jimmie Davis (left) of Louisiana wrote one of the most enduring standards of the century: "You Are My Sunshine" (right).

You are my Sunshine
Jimmie Davis

1. Verse: The other night dear as I lay sleeping
I dreamed I held you in my arms,
When I awoke dear I was mistaken,
and I hung my head and cried.

Chorus
you are my sunshine, my only sunshine
you make me happy, when skies are gray,
you'll never know dear, how much I love you,
Please don't take my sunshine away.

2. I'll always love you and make you happy,
If you will only say the same,
But if you leave me to love another,
you'll regret it all some day.
Cho

3. you told me once Dear, you Really loved me
that no one else could come between,
But now you've left me and love another,
You have shattered all my dreams.
Cho

This Land Is Your Land

WOODY GUTHRIE

(Archive Photos)

Nora Guthrie, Woody's daughter, is still the caretaker of her father's voluminous papers.

The story goes, this song was originally called "God Blessed America," as a take on the song "God Bless America" by Irving Berlin.

It was just a response to the lack of attention the government was giving to people in need during the Depression and afterwards. So here was the very popular "God Bless America"; this song was really his response to Irving Berlin's false optimism. It was so obvious that God hadn't blessed America for everybody.

Now, on the original rough draft—Woody had very good handwriting, actually.

He had gorgeous handwriting. Well, he was a writer. We've got thousands and thousands of pages of that handwriting. We have an amazing number of songbooks and books. He seemed to have a ton of fun, like a young guy putting together these songbooks of his. He would write all the lyrics of all the songs that he had ever written, and then he'd take tradi-

tional tunes and scratch out the lyrics and write his own. So there was that kind of playfulness, like a young guy in the thirties would have: "This is my work. This is the bulk of my work here."

It's an inspired song; you can hear the inspiration in it.

The song has been done by so many people under so many different circumstances that it doesn't really hit people that it's actually a very personal song. He went from California to the New York island. It wasn't like he was sitting in a chair somewhere having a vision of traveling. Everything in that song is true. It's not a vision, although it ended up being a visionary song.

It's a very poignant, political song, and it's been watered down a lot, but maybe that's not in our control. People feel it and sing it for a lot of different reasons, but so be it. The only restriction we have on that song is that it can't be used in a political campaign. It's not a politician's song; it's really the people's song.

Dylan did a lot of Woody's songs, didn't he?

Yeah, though he didn't record that many; most of his recordings are his own stuff. But he knew every Woody song; he became the first person who imitated everything Woody did. Woody would tease him and say, "You sound more like me than I do." It was strange, though, because when Dylan came around in the early sixties, Woody was already pretty advanced in Huntington's Disease, and Dylan picked that up. That [voice] became his trademark. And my mother used to go nuts. She used to tell Bob, "The most beautiful thing about Woody when he performed [in the old days] was that you could understand every word he said." Who would have known that's why Dylan was so popular? And then Tom Petty and others started dragging their notes. It was a very funny continuation.

178
W

God Blessed America

This Land Was made for You + me

This land is your land, this land is my land
From California to the New York Island,
From the Redwood Forest, to the Gulf stream waters,
    God blessed America for me.

As I went walking that ribbon of highway
And saw above me that endless skyway,
And saw below me the golden valley, I said:
    God blessed America for me.

I roamed and rambled, and followed my footsteps
To the sparkling sands of her diamond deserts,
And all around me, a voice was sounding:
    God blessed America for me.

Was a big high wall there that tried to stop me
A sign was painted said: Private Property.
But on the back side it didn't say nothing –
    God blessed America for me.

When the sun come shining, then I was strolling
In wheat fields waving, and dust clouds rolling;
The voice was chanting as the fog was lifting:
    God blessed America for me.

One bright sunny morning in the shadow of the steeple
By the Relief office I saw my people –
As they stood hungry, I stood there wondering if
    God blessed America for me.

* all you can write is
what you see.

Woody G.
N.Y., N.Y., N.Y.
Feb. 23, 1940
43rd st & 6th Ave.,
Hanover House

original copy
of this song

Used by permission, The Woody Guthrie Archive.

Save the Last Dance for Me

Sharyn Felder is the daughter of Doc Pomus, who with Mort Shuman wrote some of the most famous songs of the late fifties and early sixties. After he died, she found among his things an invitation to his own wedding, where he'd scrawled the beginnings of what would become one of the great wedding songs of all time—"Save the Last Dance for Me."

Do you remember your father writing songs around the house?

My father was writing until the week he died. He never stopped writing. He scribbled on everything—napkins, whatever he had.

Tell me a little about his background.

He came from Brooklyn, a poor family. They were a little bit different; his father was a lawyer and a politician, but he wasn't a rich lawyer; he was more like the neighborhood lawyer. They were always struggling, so they lived in a walk-up in Williamsburg.

What was his style? When you were a little kid, did he have a separate room he stayed in at the piano?

During the heyday of the Brill Building era, when he was a Brill Building songwriter, he maintained an office in Manhattan and he was very disciplined.

His entire life was disciplined for songwriting, and if he had an assignment he would lock himself up in a hotel room across the street. He was given a penthouse at the Brill Building, but he hated being in such a fancy setting, so he asked for a dive instead and moved to a smaller room. His inspiration came from when things were funkier and rougher, and there were no fancy distractions in the way.

Do you know what inspired "Save the Last Dance for Me," besides the wedding itself?

I think he was trying to make it sound a little bit like a Spanish translation. He said nobody would actually say "in whose arms you're gonna be." He wanted it to sound like it was translated from a Latin-tinge song, Spanish to English. If you listen to the lyrics you'll hear that some of the lines sound like they're not correct grammar, and he did that intentionally.

How did you find it?

After he died, among his things. It was nothing that I had ever known about before. Nobody noticed it.

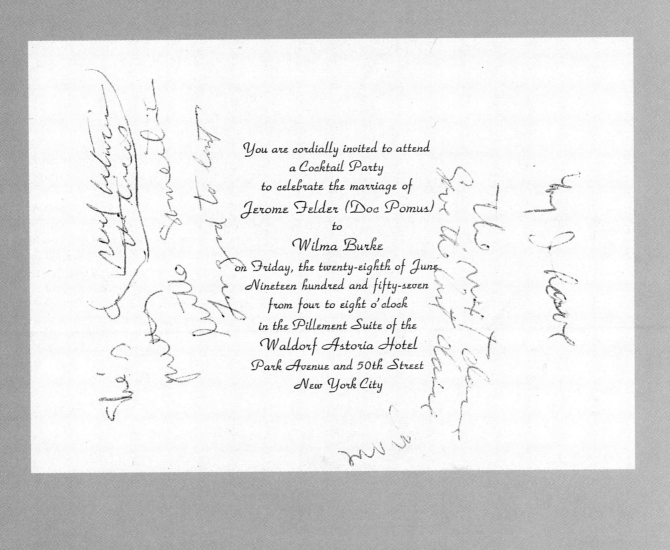

You are cordially invited to attend
a Cocktail Party
to celebrate the marriage of
Jerome Felder (Doc Pomus)
to
Wilma Burke
on Friday, the twenty-eighth of June
Nineteen hundred and fifty-seven
from four to eight o'clock
in the Pillement Suite of the
Waldorf Astoria Hotel
Park Avenue and 50th Street
New York City

Heartbreak Hotel

ELVIS PRESLEY

Elvis in the studio, 1956.
(Archive Photos)

*M*ae Boren Axton writes:

My friendship with Elvis Presley began when he was still a teenager. A deejay friend of mine from Memphis, Bob Neal, became Elvis's first manager. Bob called me in Jacksonville, Florida, for help in getting Elvis to appear in shows in the state. When I did, I saw how special he was—how people of all ages, especially teenagers, reacted with tears and screams for this then-unknown singer.

As a firsthand observer of this phenomenon, I told Elvis that all he needed was a million-seller, and I was going to write it for him. I kept trying to think of the right angle. One evening one of my good friends and co-writer, Tommy Durden, came to my house with a small article from the newspaper about a well-dressed, middle-aged man who had committed suicide, leaving a note that said, "I walk a lonely street."

I was stunned. I said, "But Tommy, everyone in the world has someone who cares, regardless of how rich or poor they are, how good or bad, how high or low their status in life. He must have been heartbroken. I'm going to put a 'Heartbreak Hotel' at the end of his lonely street."

"That's a great idea. Let's write it."

I took a legal pad and started writing, and Tommy started singing as I wrote. Twenty-two minutes later it was on tape, and I called Elvis in Memphis and told him, "Elvis, I've just written your first number one record." At the time he was just being signed to RCA Victor. He hadn't had any national hits.

"What's the name of the song?" he asked.

"It's called, 'Heartbreak Hotel,'" I said.

"Well, Mae, that's the worst song title I've ever heard. That's terrible."

"No, you're gonna love it," I said.

Tommy and I found a singer named Glenn Reaves, a honky-tonk piano player who used to mock Elvis in his own act, making him the first Elvis impersonator. We got Glenn to record a demo of the song and to really ham it up like Elvis. On the rough draft of the song we wrote, "Get Glenn R. to demo—Shaky like Elvis."

I called Elvis in Memphis and told him to meet me in Nashville—I would be flying in with Elvis's first million-seller! They met me at my hotel, and I played Elvis and Bob the tape of the song. They were smiling and Elvis said, "Hot dog, Mae, play it again. I like it, I like it!"

6

Heartbreak Hotel

Since my baby left me I've found ~~a new place~~
~~a new place~~ to dwell
~~I walk down a lonely street~~
~~It's~~ Down at the end of "Lonely Street" to
HEARTBREAK HOTEL
and I'm so lonely -- I'm so lonely, I'm
so lonely I could die
~~And if it seems too crowded~~
And tho'
~~Although~~ ~~And tho~~ it's always crowded you still can find
Some room
For broken-hearted lovers to cry there in the
and be Gloom
~~Where~~ they're so lonely oh so lonely, oh so
lonely -- they could die; flowering
~~The bell-hop's tears keep flowing~~ ~~stream~~
The desk clerk's dressed in black
They've been so long on "Lonely Street" they'll
never no never go back
And they're so lonely, oh they're so lonely
They're so lonely they pray to die

Well, if your baby leaves you, and you've?
~~my~~ ~~me~~
have
~~got~~ a tale to tell
Just take a walk down "Lonely Street"
to HEARTBREAK HOTEL
where you'll be ~~so~~ lonely and I'll be lonely
will be so lonely, we could
die

For E.P.
October 1955   By Mae Boren Axton
Tommy Durden

Idea-
Suicide
note Tommy
saw "I walk down
a lonely street."

Get
Glenn R. to demo
Shaky Elvis

Bye Bye Love/Wake Up Little Susie

THE EVERLY BROTHERS

(Archive Photos)

Felice Bryant wrote many of the Everly Brothers' hits with her husband.

Your husband, Boudleaux—he wrote songs for fun?

He didn't do it for fun; he did it for me, because we had no money. He couldn't buy me anything; he couldn't take me to a show; he couldn't take me to dinner.

He knew it made you happy.

It made me totally and completely happy. That's what I did as a child—I wrote. I'd write stories and I'd write songs to old Italian music.

Once you both started being very successful, did you still write together?

There was a time when the requests were coming in, and he'd hack them out by himself on the way down to the session. When someone would say, "Boudleaux, do you have a tune for so and so?" and he'd say, "Yeah, man, I'll bring it right down." And he'd write it in the car, on the way down. Never said he didn't have a song.

He just had a natural talent for it.

Oh, shoot! I'd sweat over lyrics; he never had to. A true poet. When Boudleaux felt he had to edit, which he had to with my stuff, he'd stay up two or three nights if something big was happening. He made sure it was a piece of perfection.

"Bye Bye Love" is such a great song. How did it get started? Did you show it to the Everly Brothers first?

Boudleaux started "Bye Bye Love." We were coming to the site where we built our lake house, and we're turning onto this dirt road, and he says, "I've got the best idea for Johnnie and Jack. It's fantastic." And I said, "Well, what is it?" And he sang the chorus. So he had that. When we wrote it, Boudleaux

thought it was ideal for a country act; he could hear the harmony—he was a harmony freak. It got turned down by a bunch of people, but Johnnie and Jack held the song and they released it. Then the Everlys came to town, and Archie Blyer of Cadence Records said, "I really believe in this, I really like this, what do you think?" And Don and Phil were ready to do anything, and they said, "Yeah, yeah, yeah, man." The others were prima donnas, but the Everlys were not. That's why they've been so big in the business. They were very kind.

Talking about "Wake Up Little Susie"— there's a section in this original rough draft, "Your daddy's gonna skin my head/When we tell him what happened he won't believe a word we've said." But this wasn't about both of you, a true story about anyone?

Well, in a way. When I was born, in the hospital they wouldn't give me a name. So the nurses started calling me Black-eyed Susan. I was covered with hair, and my mother was frightened: "Oh my God, a monkey!" And then the hair washed off and I had this long head of hair. Well, when Boudleaux and I met, he told me about his grandmother Susan, who was Indian and had long black hair, and the grandfather wanted to dig her up so that he could touch her hair again. She'd been dead for ten years or so when he'd yell up to me, "Wake up, little Susie, wake up!" And one morning, he's hitting the guitar and saying, "Wake up, little Susie," and I said "My God, that sounds great," and I ran down to get in on it.

(Archive Photos)

Bye Bye Love
Felice and Boudleaux Bryant

Bye Bye Love Bye Bye happiness
Hello Lonpliness
  I think I'm gonna cry
Bye Bye love
  " " sweet caress
Hello emptiness
  I feel like I could die
  Bye Bye ^{my} love Bye Bye

sweetheart
There goes my baby with someone new
She sure looks happy I sure am blue
~~I thought~~ she loved me - She ~~didn't~~ care

She was my baby - Til he stepped in
Goodby to romance That might have been

   free from
I'm through with romance I'm through with love
 " " " " countin' the stars above
& here's the reason—that I'm so free

Wake Up Little Susie   Boudleaux Bryant
Felice Bryant

Wake up ^{little} Susie   Wake up
Wake up Susie   " "

We've both been sound asleep
weep   Wake up little susie and weep
heap   The movies over It's four oclock
leap   And we're in trouble deep
Wake up little Susie

Susie open up your eyes
Your in for a big surprise

What are we gonna tell your mama
" " " " " " pa
What are we gonna " our friends
When they say Ooh la la
Wake Up Susie

Cut by Everly Bros   Cadence
Boudleaux Bryant   Monument
Joe Melson   Hickory
A.R. R & B record — Merc. 1967
A.R. 10   Riverboat Soul Band Merc. 1967

The movie wasn't so hot
It didn't have much of a plot
We fell asleep

Your fathers gonna be hot
likely me likely as not
The truth won't matter
our goose is cooked
Our reputation is shot

{ We told your mama that i'd wed be
  I told you i'd have you in by ten

Well Susie baby looks like we goofed again

Wake Up little Susie

We Gotta Go Home

Hello Mary Lou, Goodbye Heart

RICKY NELSON

(Archive Photos/Frank Driggs)

Gene Pitney, famous for "Town Without Pity," was also a great sixties songwriter.

You've written so many songs that are classics, like "He's a Rebel."

I looked for the rough draft of "Rebel," and that's not there. But a lot of my others got saved by my mom. I would leave stuff in a suitcase; I'd take my clothes out and all this other stuff would be spirited away into a room, and I never realized what she had until she passed away and we found boxes upon boxes.

Was there an actual Mary Lou?

No, that's another funny story. I own a beach club near my house, and one night a couple of years ago I saw a guy whose face I knew from school. This guy waited all night long and finally came up to me and said, "You've got to tell me something I've always wanted to know." This is twenty-eight years later. " 'Hello Mary Lou'—that was about Mary Lou Stillett, wasn't it?" And I hated to tell the guy she had nothing to do with it. It was because

Mary Lou rhymed with "I love you." Kinda broke the guy's heart.

I wrote that in my 1935 Ford Coupe. It had a rumble seat; candy-apple red with a white Orlon top. I used to go out to this little pond with my guitar and sit there, and that's where I wrote the song with a guitar. I had the phrase—the phrase was in my head. "Hello Mary Lou, goodbye heart." Then I had to create the rest of it around that.

It's interesting that you had so many hits as a singer that you didn't write—and yet you're a great songwriter.

It's very strange. I'm not a traveling writer. I think most people are. They get inspired by being on boats and trains and planes. I still have to go and lock myself in a room and commit myself to songwriting. The minute I started having success as an artist, myself, that kind of blew out the songwriting.

"HELLO MARY LOU, GOODBYE HEART"

WORDS & MUSIC
BY
GENE PITNEY

HELLO MARY LOU, GOODBY HEART,

SWEET MARY LOU, I'M SO IN LOVE WITH YOU,

I KNEW MARY LOU, WE'D NEVER PART,

SO HELLO MARY LOU, GOODBY HEART,

    YOU PASSED ME BY, ONE SUNNY DAY,

    FLASHED THOSE BIG, BROWN EYES MY WAY,

    AND ooh ~~I KNEW~~ I WANTED YOU FOREVER MORE,

    THEN ~~~~ *someone* SAID, "GIVE IT A WHIRL",   *Now I'm not that get's around*

    I'LL INTRODUCE YOU TO THAT GIRL,   *I swear My feet ~~~~ stuck to the groun*

    AND THO' I NEVER DID MEET YOU BEFORE,

(I SAID)
HELLO MARY LOU, GOODBY HEART,

SWEET MARY LOU, I'M SO IN LOVE WITH YOU,

I KNEW MARY LOU, WE'D NEVER PART,

SO HELLO MARY LOU, GOODBY HEART,

    I saw your lips, I heard your voice,

    ~~~~ *Believe me I just no choice,*

    ~~~~ *wild horses couldn't make me stay away,*

    BUT TO ASK YOU FOR A DATE THE VERY NEXT DAY,

    I thought about a moonlit night,

    WHEN I CALLED YOU ON THE PHONE,

    My arms around you goodn' tight,

    AND YOU ANSWERED AT YOUR HOME,

    That's all I had to see for me to say,

    THERE WAS ONLY ONE THING I COULD SAY,

Hey Hey
(~~I SAID~~)
HELLO MARY LOU, GOODBY HEART,

SWEET MARY LOU, I'M SO IN LOVE WITH YOU,

I KNEW MARY LOU, WE'D NEVER PART,

SO HELLO MARY LOU, GOODBY HEART,

Runaway

DEL
SHANNON

Shirley Westover was Del Shannon's wife.

I guess you two met early on.

I was fifteen, and I went to see *Gone With the Wind,* and while we were in the theater Charles [Westover—Del Shannon's real name] came in and sat behind us and kind of was teasing us and wanted an introduction. I didn't like him at first, but I married him at seventeen.

What were some of the ways that Del would write songs?

I know we'd go for drives a lot. He would have me drive, and he would just sit with his guitar and he would get ideas from road signs, just a lot of different ideas. He always loved country music, and country was always so sad, you know. He'd watch peoples' lives to get ideas.

How did the song "Runaway" come about? Who came up with the title?

Actually, he was working at the Hi-Lo Club down in Battle Creek, Michigan, with Max Crook, his organ player. If you notice, on the credit he gave Max half the song because Max was just kind of playing around with the organ and hit a couple of notes, and Chuck [Del] said, "Oh, stop, stop, play that again," and that's how "Runaway" began. And the owner got very upset with them, because for hours they just sat there and worked on that song while they were getting paid to be entertaining people.

When did he begin fooling around with that falsetto he used on "Runaway"?

Oh, Lord, you know, I couldn't tell you. He always kind of threw his voice, because when I first met him he was singing a lot of country music and yodeling and things like that, so I think he was always kind of messing around with it. He really did like country, and we were probably more in hopes of him going country. But in those days, of course, you'd have to sell an awful lot of records to make any money, and he was just determined that he wasn't going to do country because you'd have to be gone a lot, and you just didn't sell many records back then as a country star.

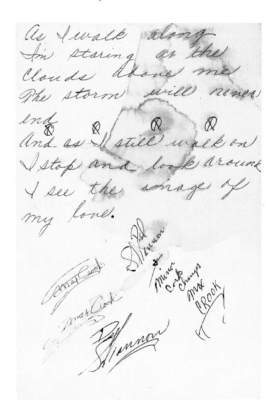

— Little Runaway —

As I walk along I wonder
what went wrong
With our love, a love
that was so strong
And as I walk along
I think of things we've
done — together when
our love was young
(BRIDGE)
I'm walking in the rain
Tears are falling and I feel a pain.

Wishing you were here by me
To end this misery
And I wonder I Wa Wa Wa, Wa Wonder
Why Why-Why-Why she ran away
And I wonder where she
will stay my little run away.

My Special Angel

JIMMY
DUNCAN

Jimmy Duncan writes:

I had just arrived in Houston from Nashville, where I had cut a record session. By the time I picked up my car at the airport and drove home, it was about two in the morning.

My lovely wife, Lily, met me at the door with a warm kiss and a sleepy hug. She took me by the arm and said, "Come to the family room. I've got something to show you." There on the couch, sound asleep, was my precious little four-year-old daughter, Sherry. "She stayed awake for you as long as she could, but she finally was so tuckered out she fell asleep." As gently as I could, I gathered her up in my arms, and halfway to her bedroom I felt her little arms slowly steal around my neck, although I knew she was still sound asleep. I laid her on her little bed, and her mother tucked her in and spread her long golden blond hair over her pillow.

As we sat holding hands, watching our baby sleep, it came into my mind: "My God, she looks just like an angel." All at once it was there. I found a composition book full of her drawings, and on a blank page, in less than ten minutes, I wrote the words to "My Special Angel." I went to the piano, and in another thirty I had the melody and an idea for the arrangement. It never crossed my mind that I had written a song that would sell countless millions of records and be played on the air more than three million times.

I thought I had written something for my special angel that I could sing for her in the morning and maybe get myself an extra hug. Something for her alone. Even now she still knows it's her song, and when they play it on the radio I still get that extra hug.

Special
"My ~~Little~~ Angel"

Special
You are my ~~Little~~ Angel,
Sent from up above,
The Lord smiled down on me,
And sent ~~my~~ an Angel to love,

Special
You are my ~~Little~~ Angel,
~~You with Heaven shone~~ Right from Paradise,
I know that you're ~~my~~ an Angel,
Heaven is in your eyes.

The smile from your lips,
Brings the summer sunshine,
The tears from your eyes bring the rain,
~~I feel your touch~~
~~I hear your voice~~, your warm embrace,
And I'm in Heaven again,

Special
You are my ~~Little~~ Angel,
Through eternity,
Special
I'll have my ~~Little~~ Angel,
Here to watch over me,

Monster Mash

BOBBY PICKETT

In the late 1950s, aspiring actor Bobby Pickett was a member of a Los Angeles group called the Cordials. Between verses of the song "Little Darlin'"—a song already graced with its share of funny vocal effects—he started doing his impression of Boris Karloff, an act he'd developed as a child. The crowd loved it.

Bobby and his friend Leonard Capizzi, the leader of the Cordials, had always loved horror movies, and they thought it'd be fun to do a horror-movie parody as a dance record. Taking off on the hip dance of the moment, the Mashed Potato, they came up with the "Monster Mash," featuring Bobby's Karloffian voice. The song became a No. 1 hit in 1962, and the singer—rechristened Bobby "Boris" Pickett—went on to claim the title of Guy Lombardo of Halloween.

Monster Mash

one
...king in the lab late ... night

... eyes beheld an ... eerie sight

... my monster ... lab began
And ... ... to my ...

He did the Mash
Boris ... did the Monster Mash

... a graveyard ...

Boris ...

... It caught on in a flash
He did ...

... he did ... Mash ... ...

Meet the Flintstones

BILL
HANNA

How did you first team up with Joe Barbera?

It goes back many years. In 1937, I was working at Harmonizing Studios, and I got a call from MGM that they were going to discontinue working with that company and start their own cartoon company, and so I went to work for them. At the same time, MGM had hired a number of people from New York. One of those was Joe Barbera. We were both working on stories, but not together at first. Joe was doing storyboards. We started working together very soon after that, working on stories. Back at Harmonizing, I'd written many lyrics to songs for animated cartoons: "It's Huckleberry Hound, the biggest clown in town, for all you guys and gals." That kind of thing.

The songwriting style of writing for animated features seems so easy, but you have to get a lot of information in the lyric in a short amount of time.

Yeah, it usually tells the story.

So you would just sit there in a chair, without a piano, and figure out the song in your head?

Yeah, that is right. I would sit there and write lyrics and, almost with the lyrics, the music. I always just went to Scott Bradley, my musician, and sang the songs. He put down the lead sheet with the song.

Did you do all the famous Hanna-Barbera themes?

I did *Yogi Bear, Huckleberry Hound, Quickdraw McGraw, The Jetsons* . . .

Some of the networks might have wanted to bring in professional songwriters to write the songs. But at that point you had the power to say, "We want to do it ourselves"?

Yes, that's right. A musician would do the arrangement for the orchestra, I didn't do that. All I did was write the lyrics and the melody.

Are you surprised by the longevity of The Flintstones?

Well, I'll tell you what. I'm not giving the music any credit here. To me, I think that the concept of the show, the format of the show, was good, and it was easy to write. The music fit the mood of the show, and I think we just, I'll say, got lucky.

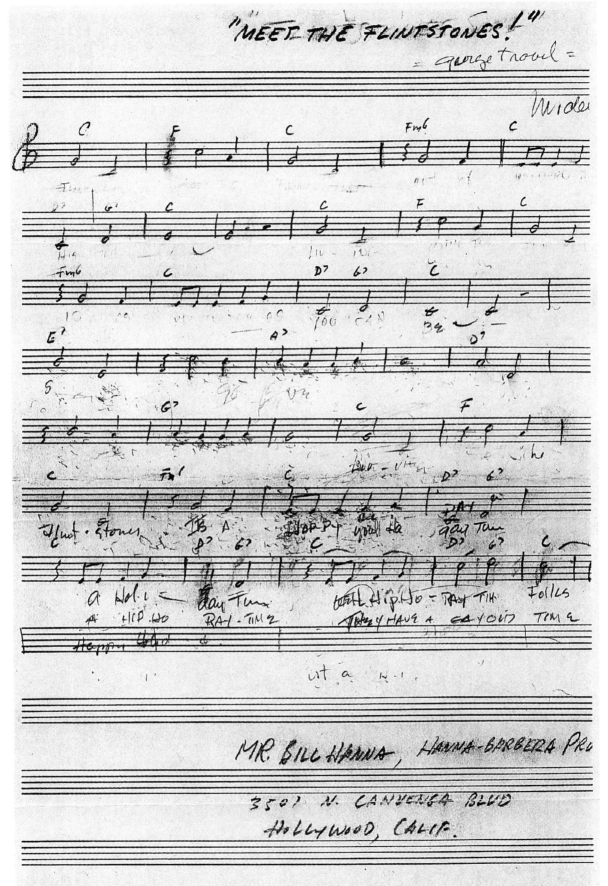

Mama Said

Willie Denson was one of the great girl-group songwriters of the early sixties.

How did you come up with the title "Mama Said"?

That's something I always used to say when things got tough. You know what I mean. I said, "Hey, Mama said there'd be days like this." So I said, hey, that's a good title for a song.

Was this the first song you wrote with Luther Dixon?

Well, you see, the way that happened—I was running around selling the music. All of these songs were on demo. At the time I took it to him, it was on demo. I sang on all the demos; there was "Mama Said" on there, and "Blue Holiday," which was the back side of "Mama Said," and another song called "Ten Below Zero." I was working nights at that time for the postal service, and when I got off in the mornings, I would take a shower, then I would play with my music.

How did you get "Mama Said" to the Shirelles?

I called Luther that day. It was snowing, and he said he needed material. So I went over there and he signed those three songs, and they were having a rehearsal that Saturday with, you know, King Curtis, who was the musical director. So they said, "Look, come over Saturday to the rehearsal hall," and he gave me the place to work. So they gave him a contract the next day. On the Shirelles' greatest hits album, I have maybe four songs.

What was it like working as a writer back then?

I used to run into Luther a lot. I didn't know him personally, but he knew me and I knew him, because it was a little circle there—Bobby Darin, Connie Francis, Carole King. I was working out of the building with Carole King. I was a staff writer, but I was the only writer for Luther, so I *was* the staff.

You mentioned that you were working some kind of job at the time.

Yeah, I'd been working at a company that made clothes. Originally I had thought of it as a work song, like a nine-to-five type song. But then I figured I would change it and make it a love thing, since that kind of thing will sell better than a work song.

And you were writing a lot at that point?

Well, yeah. I got my first copyright while I was in grade school. It was actually one of those things where you send off, you know, song poems, and you pay money to set the music to it. But I found out that was a racket, you know what I mean. I mean, I was like thirteen or fourteen years old, but I was proud. I was like, hey, this is my first copyright. You know, I got it in Washington, D.C., and I was showing it to all the kids in school.

Mama Said

C

Mama said there'd be days
Like this. There'd be days
Like this mama said.
Mama said there'd be days Like
this. There'd be days Like this
mama said.

I went walking the other day
every thing was going fine. I
met a little girl named Mary Jo—
I almost lost my mind,

Repeat C

I'm On My Way

RANDY NEWMAN

When you were, say, eleven or twelve years old, walking around the house, what kind of music would your mom and dad have on?

Nothing in the home. It was on the car radio. When I was eleven and twelve, rock 'n' roll was just starting; we had a black woman who came to clean our house, and that was how I first heard "Sh-boom" and "Shake, Rattle and Roll" and, you know, the Bill Haley stuff.

Not many people would say their influences were Stephen Foster or ragtime. Did you actually listen to them?

No, it wasn't a conscious thing. I think I always liked those four-square, diatonic tunes somehow. You know, like "There's a Long, Long Trail A-Winding" is one of my favorite songs—it's a World War I song. I never listened to Stephen Foster particularly. I've never heard Professor Longhair or anything, I've only heard it through Fats Domino, whom I love, and through New Orleans stuff: "Sea Cruise" and "Let the Good Times Roll."

I'm a big fan; I know all your albums. How did your songwriting get to such a point, where you're able to express this combination of self-effacing humor coupled with depression?

Probably due to shyness to some degree—and that so much of what I write is in the third person. You know, I think I'm hesitant about saying things like "I love you." I've never been happy about writing; I like having written something, but I was just never eager about the task.

The song you sent me, "I'm On My Way"—you wrote on the back that it was in an old U.C.L.A. notebook. "See what comprehensive notes I took," you said, and then it's dated 1964—May 25.

Jesus, it has the date on it. I don't remember it. It's old. So I was twenty.

I'll read you some of the lyrics: "Nothing's gonna stand in my way/Gonna be a big man someday/So just step aside or get on and ride/'Cause I'm rollin', I'm rollin', I'm on my way."

Yeah, Billy Joel did a little better fifteen years ago. But it's a young man's song.

(Archive Photos)

I'm On My Way

Nothin's gonna stand in my way
Gonna be a big man someday
So just step aside
Or get on and ride,
Cause I'm rollin' I'm rollin
I'm On My Way

I don't care, what you say
You think I can't do it but I'll find a way
And when I do, I'll be laughin' at you
I can take it, 'cause I knew I'm gonna make it
I'm On My Way

I ain't ever had a thing
But I'm gonna change that Past
Feel so good that I could sing
(Cause I'm on the road at last)

Now I can't let anyone
Get in my
Slow me down until the job is done
So get out of my way
I got no time to play
Cause I'm rollin', Girl Baby I'm rollin
Girl I'm on My Way

11 2 01

PART TWO

Sunshine Days

GOOD DAY SUNSHINE

(16E) INTRO (Breaks etc...)

◯ —————— GOOD DAY SUNSHINE

① I need to laugh, and when the sun is out
I've got something I can laugh about

② I feel good in a special way
I'm in love and it's a summy day,

CHORUS ———— GOOD DAY SUNSHINE

③ We take a walk, the sun is shining down
Burns my feet as they touch the ground.

D.
G.

~~Verse~~ Good Day Sunshine. (Breaks etc..)

④ Then we lie beneath a shady tree,
I love her, and she's loving me.

⑤ She feels good, she knows she's looking fine
I'm so proud to know that she is mine,

◯ ———— Good Day Sunshine (FORTE)
                              (PIANO)

Good
Good

Length 2·10 ohyeh

In Penny Lane there was a barber
                        showing photographs
Of every head he'd had the pleasure to know
It was easy not to go - he was very slow

Meanwhile back ~~Penny Lane~~ behind the shelter
in the middle of the round about
A pretty nurse is selling poppies from a tray
And though she feels as if she's in a play
She is anyway.

In Penny Lane the barber shaves another customer
We see the banker sitting for a trim
And then the fireman rushes in
From the pouring rain - very strange

Penny Lane is in my ears and in my eyes
There beneath the blue suburban skies
And meanwhile back at.
~~Penny Lane is in my ears and in my eyes~~
~~There beneath the blue suburban skies / Penny Lane~~

Lonely Rita, Meter maid,
Nothing can come between us,
When did you start to ~~you~~ tow your heart
(.. it gets dark till) away....

Standing by a parking meter
When I caught a glimpse of Rita
                all
(writing ~~down~~ the numbers in her little)
                            black book)
Filling in a ticket with her little
                blue pen.

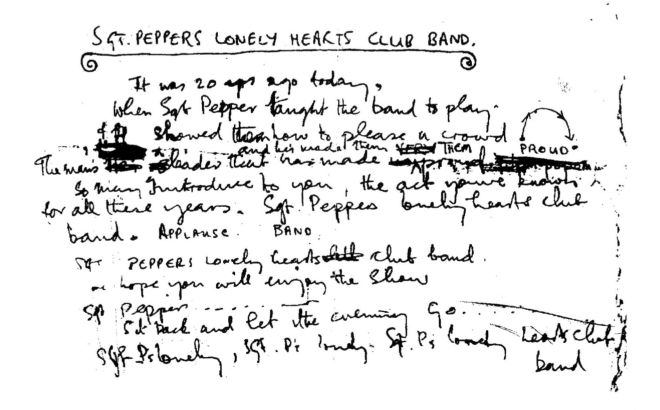

An early sketch for the Sgt. Pepper *sleeve, with some notes for "Lucy in the Sky with Diamonds" and "She's Leaving Home."*
Below, "Pepper" itself.

Sunshine Superman

DONOVAN

When you were first getting into music, would you buy records and just sit around and listen?

Well, I grew up in Gloucester. Now, in the forties and fifties, television and radio hadn't really become what they are today, and people still sang Irish and Scottish songs at parties. A lot of Irish influence. My father was a reader of monologues and can still memorize enormous amounts of poetry. It's a traditional talent of the Celts. And then, when I was fourteen, what did I hear? Buddy Holly. That was an amazing event in my life. I had heard Bill Haley and I had heard Elvis, but in my age group, I suppose, it was really when I heard Buddy Holly.

Now, something like "Sunshine Superman" looks like it was in a little book. Did you used to have a little songbook?

Yeah, I've got loads of songbooks, all different shapes and sizes, and none of them are complete. I was never that organized. But they're all there. Some books just have half a dozen or so in one and two in the other, and maybe loads of drawings and things like that.

Did you keep anything else?

I found other songs, but some of them are illegible, because maybe you're sort of scribbling half in the dark, lying in some house of mine or flat or hotel room. "Sunshine Superman"—although it sounds like Latin jazz, there was a Beatles influence there. The images come from pop art of the day. I was studying painting in college, and I thought I was going to be a painter. That's why so many of my songs have colors in them. There was a comics store, when I was ten, across the tram tracks in Glasgow, and I was an avid comic collector: Green Lantern and Superman. Of course, the Superman relates to the superman of the mind, that Nietzsche and Buddhism speak of—the superhuman inside us all. But all those images were fun to write about. "Sunshine Superman" was for Linda; she was my muse and still is. We had split up for a period, and that song was a kind of letter to her. And so we married, and so that human aspect of the song is very strong. And so Linda Lawrence is now Linda Leach. "Sunshine Superman" is still a favorite; I sing it when I perform. I love the way it's structured; I also tried to write others like it, and it's very odd: It doesn't work that way for me. I can't do it.

After writing "Sunshine Superman," you got into a serious Bohemian thing.

Oh, yeah. We were going to travel the world. The whole idea was just to make enough money to travel—to go to India, to South America, to really just follow the path of Jack Kerouac. I would go away from England with my pack and my guitar. I had the gypsy bug. So I was sittin' up there on the mountains in Greece, eating tomatoes, Greek cheese, big bottles of wine, and writing songs. This was in 1966. So we went down to take a phone call, and we're listening on the phone through Athens, through Paris to London, and it was my manager, and he said, "You better get your ass back here, man, 'Sunshine Superman' is number one in the United States. And it was like when Buddy Holly got the call—do you know that story? He didn't even know the record had been released.

Sunshine came softly
through my
window today
could have tripped out
easy but I've
changed ma way
it'll take time I know it
but in a while
you're gonna be mine
I know it
we'll do it in style
Co I've made my
mind up your going
to be mine
any trick in the book
now baby
that I can find

Superman an' Green
Lantern ain't got
nothin' on me
I can make like
a turtle an' dive for
pearls in the sea
~~4 you can~~
thinkin' of a
velvet throne
bout all the rainbows
you can
have for your own
Co I've made my
mind up your
going to be mine
any trick in the book
your baby
that I can find.

Everybody hustlein
~~just to they can~~
have a little scene
~~We stood on a beach~~
~~at sunset~~
~~you know~~
when I say we'll be
cool I think ~~that~~ you
know ~~just~~ what I mean
We ~~stood~~ on a beach
at sunset
d'you remember when
~~I wanted to stay~~
There is a beach I know
where
the ~~sun~~ it never ends
~~when~~ you made
your mind up forever
to be mine
I'll pick up your hand
an slowly
blow your mind

Co I've made my
mind up you going
to be mine
any trick in the book
your baby that
I can find

Ferry Cross the Mersey

GERRY AND THE PACEMAKERS

Stephen Bishop interviewed Gerry Marsden.

I've been trying to get in touch with you for some time, because I always thought you wrote such great songs. I've always been a fan. Do you have any kind of rough of "Don't Let the Sun Catch You Crying"?

I just have things on paper and bits of odds and ends, you see. But I'll certainly look around and see what I can find.

"Don't Let the Sun Catch You Crying" I wrote for my girlfriend; we'd had an argument, and she said, "Right, we're finished." And I thought, bloody hell, how can I get her to come back? So I wrote "Don't Let the Sun Catch You Crying," and I sent it to her on a tape. She listened to it and said "Gerry, let's get back together again." And that young girl is now my wife.

"Ferry Cross the Mersey" was written for a film we made, and for a long time, trying to write it, I couldn't think of an idea or get the feel of a ferryboat. I was taking my girlfriend out for dinner, and suddenly I got a line in my head, *doo, doo, doo, doo.* So I stopped the car, jumped out, and got on the phone to my house, told them put the tape deck near the phone, and hummed it—just hummed the intro down the phone line. Got back into the car, dropped my wife back at her house, said, "Sorry, no dinner tonight," went back to my home, and wrote the song within five minutes. The whole song.

Well, your wife should get some of the royalties.

Don't worry, she gets them anyway.

FERRY CROSS THE MERSEY J.M.

INTRO: De — Do De De Do, DA — De Do Do SLIDE BASS STRING
I am B DOWN TO E OPEN

Life goes on DAy AfTeR DAy
HEARTS TORN in EVERY way So
FERRY CROSS THe Mersey Cos THIS LANDS THe PLACE I LOVE
AND HERE ILL STAY

(circled) ✓ JUST IN CASE

People WITH LOVE EVER THERE ✳ (struck through)

PEOPLE THEY RUSH EVE here
EACH WITH THEIR OWN SECRET CARE
So FERRY CROSS THe Mersey and Always TAKE ME There
The PLACE I LOVE.

PEOPLE AROUND EVEry CORNER
SEEM TO SMILE AND SAY
WE DONT CARE WHERE YOU COME FROM ✳ (struck through)
WE DONT CARE WHAT YOUR NAME IS BOY
WE'LL NEVER TURN YOU AWAY ✳

So I'LL CONTINUE TO SAY
HERE I ALWAYS WILL STAY
So FERRY CROSS THe Mersey Cos THIS LANDS
AND HERE ILL STAY The PLACE I LOVE

" " " " " " " "

END KEY OF E SLOW.
FAIRLY

This Diamond Ring

GARY LEWIS
AND THE
PLAYBOYS

(Archive Photos/Frank Driggs)

Al Kooper, late of "Like a Rolling Stone" and Blood, Sweat and Tears fame (he played Hammond organ on the former, and founded the latter), co-wrote Gary Lewis's mid-sixties hit.

"This Diamond Ring" must have been written about 1964 or 1965?

I would think 1962 or 1963.

That early?

Yeah. It didn't come out until later, but we wrote it in 1962 or 1963. We wrote it for the Drifters.

Did you do a demo of it back then?

We did. It was a black demo. My friend Jimmy Radcliff sang the demo.

When you look back at that now, how do you feel about it? Do you feel proud of it?

I always hated the Gary Lewis record, because it was an R&B song and they took all the soul out of it. Later, I cut it on an album of mine, and I cut it the way it was written.

I still love the original record, though—I thought it was very hip, had a special vibe to it.

I just can't stand it. It was very summer, very California. It was an unbelievably white record. They played the shit out of it when it was number one; it knocked "You've Lost That Lovin' Feeling" out of number one, and then "Eight Days a Week" knocked it out.

So who came up with the idea?

I was writing with Bob Brass and Irwin Levine. I don't recall who came up with the idea; I just know that at that time we were writing two or three songs a day—you know, Tin Pan Alley.

So when you guys were doing the song, were you playing keyboards or guitar? How were you set up to write, do you remember?

I was at the piano and one of them was on each side, and we would just bash it out.

When you wrote it, did you think it would be a hit?

Yeah, I said, "God, if we could just get the Drifters on this, it would be fantastic." And I was kinda excited about it, because I really liked the modulations in it. I thought they were very clever. Try and play it—it's weird. It's very advanced for a twenty-one-year-old.

Who wants to buy this diamond ring?
She took it off her finger now it
doesn't mean a thing.

This diamond ring doesn't shine
for me anymore.
and this diamond ring doesn't mean
what it meant before.
So if you've got someone
whose love is true
Let it can shine for you

This stone is genuine like love
should be
And if you're baby's true then
My baby was to me then

this diamond can be something
beautiful
this diamond ring can be
dreams that are coming true
then your heart won't have to
break like mine did.
if this love before it

Psychotic Reaction

*J*ohn Byrne of the Count Five writes:

I was searching for the proverbial "hook line." The words "I feel depressed, I feel so bad, 'cause you're the best girl that I've ever had" were rolling around in my head. The line contradicted itself and I tried to change it, but the words wouldn't go away. How could I feel so bad when she was the best girl I've ever had? The next line made sense and tied it together: "I can't get your love, I can't get a fraction" [a fraction of love, that is]. That was as far as I had written. There was nothing to it—a prosaic piece of Teenage Love Drivel. But where was the hook line?

Because of the prevalence of the use of LSD and marijuana, some of my friends urged me to give the song a drug con-

notation. Unfortunately, that's what happened, and to this day people still associate the song with the hippie drug culture of the sixties.

Still, there was no hook line. I put the song aside and continued to write other songs. The rest of the Count Five—Roy, John, Butch, and Kenn—were excellent musicians. Each of them did their own part on the Song Without a Hook Line. I was sitting in a health education class in college, and the professor was discussing various mental disorders—psychosis, neurosis. The guy sitting next to me turned to me and said, "You know what would be a great title for a song? 'Psychotic Reaction'!"

I had my hook line.

I feel depressed I feel so bad
you're the best girl I've ever had
I can't get your love, no I can't get a
faction
Oh! the result in psychiatic reaction

I feel lonely aright today
I can't get near you I must stay away
I feel so good when I'm by your side
Say little girl would you like to take a ride
When I'm by your side I get satisfaction
When I'm on my own psychiatic reaction.

This Old Heart of Mine

This old heart of mine
Been broke a thousand times
Each time you break away
I fear you're gone to stay
Lonely nights — they come
The memories — they flow
Bringing you back again
Hurting me more and more

Maybe it's my mistake to show the
Love I feel inside
'Cause each day that passes by
You got me never knowing if I'm
Coming or going
But I love you - this old heart is weak for you
yes I do - yes I do
② These "old" arms of mine
Miss having you around
Makes these tears inside
Come pouring down

Always with half a kiss
You remind me of what I miss
Tho' I try to control myself
Like a fool I start grinning
Cause my head starts spinning
Cause I love you
This old heart is weak for you
I love you yes, I do yes I do.

(over)

Sylvia Moy co-wrote the Isley Brothers' 1966 hit, "This Old Heart of Mine."

③ I TRY hARD To hide
~~My~~ HURT iNSiDe
this old heart OF MiNE Always Keeps Me CRyiNG
~~Also~~ the WAy you tReAt'N Me
LeAves Me iNcomplete
You're Here FoR ~~t~~ the DAy GoNe FoR ~~the~~ the week

But iF you LeAve ~~Me~~ Me A HuNDReD times
A HuNDReD Times I'LL tAKe you BACK
I'M yourS whenever you WANT Me
I'M Not ~~too~~ Too proud to Shoot it
TeLL the WORLD About it
'CAuSe I Love you
This oLD heARt   iS WeAK FoR you
I Love you   yes I Do.   yes I Do.

Surf's Up

Brian Wilson remembers writing some of the great songs of the 1960s.

When you were a kid, what was the first song you can remember that you really liked?

I would have to say "Sh-boom." Yeah, and then the real big shocker of them all, "Rock Around the Clock." That totally turned my lights on, you know.

You must have started writing when you were really young. Were you in high school?

No, I wrote my first song when I was nineteen years old. I'd sort of got into Chuck Berry, and he stuck in my mind—he pioneered those surf melodies. And then I took his style and extrapolated on it, you know, expanded on it.

I started playing the piano when I was ten or eleven, and my uncle Charlie taught me how to play the boogie-woogie, in the key of C. It was fun. I really got off on it. And I learned how to play Chuck Berry rhythms with my left hand at the keyboard. When I say the piano, forget it—the whole world turns into a song.

Did you ever use music to help you meet girls?

Not really, but I'll tell you one thing. The guys that were at Hawthorne High School with me were extremely competitive people. After I graduated from high school, I took a lot of shit with me, the competitive shit.

Did everyone around you know that you guys were already into music?

Well, yeah. Once, Mike Love and I and two other guys at Hawthorne did a song called "Bermuda Shorts." And then later we expanded—I mean, we had "Surfin' " and "Surfer Girl." I wrote "Surfer Girl" before I wrote "Surfin'."

When you write, what are the tools you like to use? Do you usually have a tape recorder on, or do you ever use a rhyming dictionary?

No, never a rhyming dictionary, but now and then I use a tape recorder.

What part of the house did you write in when you were still at the house? Did you write in your room?

Oh no. There was a music room that was like a garage my dad had converted. There was a hi-fi and a piano and an organ in there, and so I'd go there every day after school. It's two steps down from the living room. Two little steps down, then you walk down a little corridor, and there's a whole beautiful piano in there. So I would get down there and sit at the piano, and I would go, "Well, this is really going to be great." Or the Four Freshmen, I'd put them on, and, oh wow, I think I know what they're saying. So I'd take that and learn on the piano verbatim what the Freshmen did—you know, their harmonies. I could pick out any harmony in the world from the Four Freshmen.

Do you ever have a block when you're trying to write?

I get that sometimes, and I'll say, 'Goddammit,' I'll cuss to myself, or I'll throw something across the room and really get it off my chest, you know. And then it's like, back to the grindstone.

What was it like working with Van Dyke Parks on "Surf's Up"?

Well, he's probably the nicest guy I've ever met. He's a very kind and courteous person, and he makes working a breeze. He is a great producer, too. That's all there is to it.

The music is almost like classical music. But the lyric—what exactly is it about? It's hard to figure out. Do you remember?

No, not really. It has pretty advanced lyrics. It's almost like poetry set to music. They were lyrics, but they're more than just that.

(Archive Photos/F. Capri/SAGA)

S U R F ' S   U P

lyrics by Van Dyke Parks
music by Brian Wilson

1) A DIAMOND NECKLACE PLAYED THE PAWN
    HAND IN HAND, SOME DRUMMED ALONG, WO
    TO A HANDSOME MAN AND BATON
    A BLIND CLASS ARISTOCRACY
    BACK THROUGH THE OPERA GLASS YOU SEE
    THE PIT AND THE PENDULUM DRAWN
    COLLUMNATED RUINS DOMINO

HORUS   CANVAS THE TOWN
        AND BRUSH THE BACKDROP
        ARE YOU SLEEPING BROTHER JOHN

2) HUNG VELVET OVERTAKEN ME
    DIM CHANDELIER AWAKEN ME
    TO A SONG DISOLVED IN THE DAWN
    THE MUSIC HALL A COSTLY BOW
    THE MUSIC ALL IS LOST FOR NOW
    TO A MUTED TRUMPETERS SWAN
    COLLUMNATED RUINS DOMINO

HORUS —

3) DOVE NESTED TOWERS THE HOUR WAS
    STRIKE THE STREET QUICKSILVER MOON
    CARRIAGE ACROSS THE FOG
    TWO STEP TO LAMP LIGHTS CELLARTUNE
    THE LAUGH'S COME HARD IN AULD LANGS SYNE

    THE GLASS was raised, the fired rose
    The fullness of the wine the dim last toasting

Daydream Believer

John Stewart wrote the Monkees' hit.

"Daydream Believer" was a big hit for the Monkees. How did you get the song to them back then?

I was friends with their producer, a guy named Chip Douglas. Chip and I had both been up for Dave Guard's job in the Kingston Trio, and I got it, but Chip and I stayed friends. So we were at a party one night up in Laurel Canyon, and he said "I'm recording the Monkees. Do you have any songs?" And I played him "Daydream Believer," and he said, "Yeah, that's it! That's great." Then I heard they were in the studio in New York. The next thing I knew, it was number one around the world.

The song was part of a trilogy called the Suburbia Trilogy.

Was it part of a play?

No, it was just a trilogy of songs about suburbia, and this was just one of the songs. The other two really never amounted to anything. In fact, I can't even remember what they were.

How did you come up with the title?

You know, it was just one of those things that just came. It wrote itself. You know, it was one of those twenty-minute songs.

On the rough draft, the lyrics read, "Now you know how funky I can be," which is so funny. On the final that came out "how happy I can be."

Yeah—which makes absolutely no sense. It was more of a Davy Jones image, I guess. It certainly didn't hurt the single.

That was pretty early for anyone to be using the word funky.

Exactly.

~~Day Dream Believer~~

If i could hide ~~under~~ the wings of

The bluebird as ~~it~~ ^{she} sings The 6 o'clock

alarm who never rings

But it rings then I rise wipe

The (sleep) out of my eyes my razors

old and it stings

Chorus:

Cheer up sleepy Jean oh what

Can it mean to a Day Dream

Believer and a Home Coming queen

white knight on his steed
Now you know how funky I can be

without a dollar
What else baby do we need.

Somebody to Love

JEFFERSON AIRPLANE

*D*arby Slick writes:

I was living with a woman named Leslie. She was working at the post office, Rincon Annex, which in those days was a haven for hippies and various intellectuals. Leslie loved rock 'n' roll but grew, I judged by her statements, jealous of the attention I was receiving. One night, I was home alone while she was working. I took some LSD and waited for her. She didn't come home. From hints she had dropped, which I hadn't understood but had registered in my memory, I knew she wasn't injured but was with someone else. At dawn, coming down from the drug and miserable about our disintegrating relationship, I sat with my guitar and wrote:

> *When the truth is found to be lies*
> *And all the joy within you dies*
> *Don't you want somebody to love?*
> *Don't you need somebody to love?*
> *Wouldn't you love somebody to love?*
> *You better find somebody to love.*

The whole song came very quickly, words and music. I had no tape recorder, and I didn't know how to write music notation, so I played it over and over for many hours, often sobbing as I tried to croak out the words. Finally, I went to sleep.

(Archive Photos/Jim Wells)

MIND FULL OF BREAD DARBY SLICK

                F#M   B   F#M
WHEN THE TRUTH IS FOUND TO BE LIES
     F#M   B   F# M
AND ALL THE JOY WITHIN YOU DIES

              A   B   B
DONT YOU WANT SOMEBODY TO LOVE
DONT YOU WANT SOMEBODY TO LOVE
         NEED A   E   B
WOULDNT YOU LOVE SOMEBOCY TO LOVE
                                F#M - B
YOU BETTER FIND SOMEBODY TO LOVE

TEARS ARE RUNNIN DOWN YOUR DRESS
YOUR FREINDS, THEY TREAT YOU LIKE A GUEST

CHORUS

THE GARDEN FLOWERS ARE DEAD
YOUR MIND IS FULL OF BREAD

CHRUS

Rocky Top

BUCK
OWENS

More with Felice Bryant, author of the Everly Brothers' hits and the country standard "Rocky Top."

"Rocky Top" is actually about a mountain, isn't it?

Yeah. There's a lot of mountains in Tennessee, and at the time Boudleaux and I wrote that song, we just coined that name. And then we came to find out a lot of places, mountains that were strictly rocky so that they couldn't grow anything on them, started calling themselves "Rocky Top." At the time, there was no place legally known as Rocky Top in the area; we coined that one.

So you guys were into geography, too.

There was a contest out of New York; they wanted to know where Rocky Top was. And the contest was supposed to start, so they thought, Well, hell, we'll go to the horse's mouth, and they came to ask us. We told them there was no such place—and they'd already started running this damn contest! So we named a place out in Williamson County, out on our farm, Rocky Top.

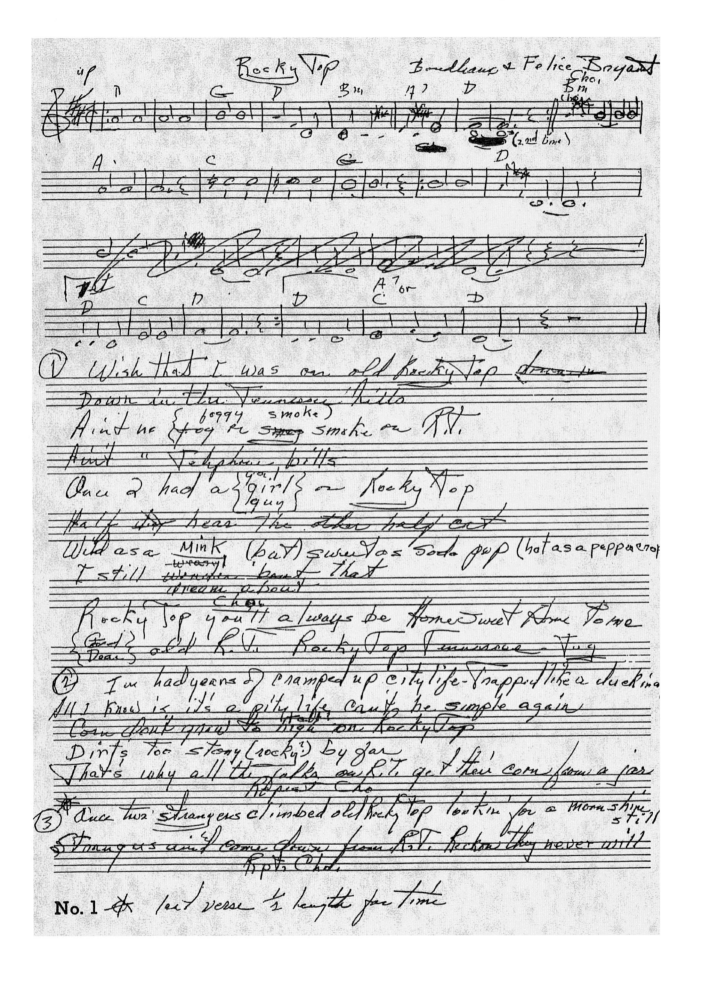

I Was Made to Love Her

STEVIE
WONDER

Stephen Bishop spoke with Sylvia Moy, co-writer of Stevie Wonder's hit.

You co-wrote "It Takes Two," "Uptight," "My Cherie Amour," "This Old Heart of Mine." How did you get into writing?

Well, I was a singer/musician, one of nine kids. Thinking in terms of going to college with very little money available, a school teacher advised me that I had something to work with, and that was my music. And the only thing I was interested in was, of course, music. But I was really trying to earn my college education. I was right out of high school and began to sing around at various functions to earn a little money, but not that much. I began asking around to find out how I could get a record deal, and I began calling record companies. They said, "Well, you'll need an original song." And I said, "Well, where do you get that?" They said, "Well, you'll have to talk to songwriters." And I began to call songwriters. Then I got into songwriting, because I couldn't get a songwriter to write anything for me, which made me kind of angry. So I sat down and did it myself, as I'd been writing songs and ditties since I was very, very young.

What was that like?

Well, we made our own instruments. We didn't have a lot of money, so we played piano on the radiator, and played with boxes and pieces of wood. Then, when I found out I was going to need a song, I sat down and listened to the radio, because I had been exposed mostly to jazz and classical music in the past. But I loved music, so I listened to the radio for about two weeks and wrote a couple of songs.

How did "I Was Made to Love Her" come about?

I was growing up out on Fleming Street in Detroit. My dad had helped a lot of his sisters and brothers and his mother and dad. A lot of them would come in from Louisiana, and I'd watch them dance every Saturday night. That country-blues kind of feeling stayed in my heart and made it into the lyrics. "I was born in Little Rock"—my mother was born near Little Rock. The influence from my parents, and the love between the two of them, definitely influenced the lyric and the melody. Now, some of the fast phrasing you hear, Stevie [Wonder] wouldn't use his braille, so I'd stand in the control room and sing a line into his earphones, and as he was singing one line he'd be hearing the next. He was amazing.

It must have been overwhelming to work with such a glowing gem of a human being.

He's a genius in his own right, and I have the utmost respect for him. There's a difference between talent and creativity. Some people are ultra-talented, and they can emulate and learn techniques, but creative people are usually very highly sensitive, and they can absorb spiritually, can feel what is going on around them and what is happening in the world. They can feel what people feel and can express it for them. I think this is often why certain records and songs and videos are popular—because they've been able to capture what is felt by human beings.

Sylvia Moy   "Party Copy"   My Man Steve Wonder

I was MADE TO LOVE HER

~~I was Made to Love Her~~ Published 4.25.6

I.

1)   I was born in Lil Rock   Steve Wo
      Had a childhood Sweetheart
~~And~~ we were Always hand in hand

cozy 2)   I wore hightop Shoes And Shirt-Tails
             Sugar was in pig-tails
sweet ~~But~~ I knew I loved her ~~too~~ even then
             You know

3)   My Papa disapproved it
      My Mama Boo-hoo hooed it
But I told them time And time Again
      Don't you know
I was Made to love her
Build My world Around her, yeah (3)

II.

She's been My inspiration
Shown   Appreciation
For the love I gave her thru the year

Like the Sweet Magnolia Tree
Oar Love Blossomed Tenderly
My life grew even Sweeter, Thru the yea.

I know My Baby Loves Me
 "   "   "   " Needs Me
Thru thick + Thin we've Made it Thro —
   + lives

Chicago

GRAHAM NASH

(Archive Photos)

What kind of music did you hear growing up?

Well, it was usually the straight stuff, Vera Lynn doing "We'll Meet Again" and all that kind of stuff, and later "Shrimpboats Are A-Coming" and "The Ballad of Davy Crockett." Then, when I was about eleven, I was listening to the American Top Forty broadcasts from Radio Luxembourg.

What was the first record that really caught your ear?

Three: "Sixteen Tons" by Tennessee Ernie Ford, "Rock Island Line" by Lonnie Donegan—

That was a big record back then. That was skiffle?

That was skiffle, yeah. And "Be Bop a Lula."

So did you start playing instruments at that point?

Yeah. All my friends had bicycles, and my mother said, "You can either have a bicycle or a guitar, but we can't afford a bicycle." So I made my first metaphysical choice.

When did you learn that you could sing higher than anyone else on the block?

Halfway through "Bye Bye Love." Don and Phil [Everly] had the melody and the tenor part taken, so there was only one place to go.

What was it like, writing with the other Hollies—Tony Hicks and Allan Clarke?

We'd just sit around playing guitars and find one line that was good—just sitting around in dressing rooms, bored.

After Crosby, Stills, and Nash formed—and then Neil Young joined—you were around so many quality songwriters. Was it ever intimidating?

No, I don't think it ever entered any of our heads to question what we were doing there. I mean, we all had a bunch of great stuff. And Neil and David [Crosby] and I had the reality rule: We would only play songs together that turned us on.

Let's talk about "Chicago." Your first venture into a political song?

Kind of, yes. There were a couple of Hollies songs that we did, one about a population explosion. But this was my first full-out, blatant, fuck-you song. Wavy Gravy called me one day, and he said that the Chicago Seven had been busted and he wanted to put on a concert to raise money for their defense funds. Me and Davey [Crosby] were right into it and wanting to go, and Stephen [Stills] and Neil [Young] didn't want to go. Either they had something else to do or they didn't believe in it or they couldn't be bothered, and that's my song to Stephen and Neil.

It's a pretty passionate song. It must have been a different adventure for you, rather than your basic love song.

Yeah, that's what David and Stephen did for me. It was okay to feel that way, and it was okay to express yourself that way because they were doing it with "Long Time Gone" and "For What It's Worth." So that made it okay for me to do it.

chicago

So your brothers bound and gagged
and they've chained him to a chair
wont you please go to chicago
                    just to sing.

In a land that preaches freedom
how can such a thing be fair
Wont you please got to Chicago
   for the help that we can bring sing.

That we can change the world
re-arrange the world is dying
                    to get better.

Polititians please go home
theres nothing for you here.
wont you please go to chicago for a ride
A simple song of justice
is all we want to hear
Wont you please go to Chicago
just to balance out the sides, really
So a simple song of freedoms what we'd want to hear
        ask to help you cod he'll turn
                    the other ear
nd you camb

You jump in front of my
(Car when you know all)
the time that 90 miles
an hour is the speed I drive

You tell me it's alright, you
~~don't mind a little pain~~
the tire tracks ~~across~~ across
your back, how do you manage
to stay alive —

Cross town traffic - so hard to get
        through to you
Cross town Traffic - I don't want run
over you.
Cross-town traffic - All you do is slow
me down - and I'm tryin' to get to
the other side of town

~~[scribbled out lines]~~

When must you always try
to prove to me . . . a ~~[crossed out]~~ skid
mark ~~across~~ your back is all
you want from me

~~I know~~ I'm not the only see
who'd accused of hit and ~~[crossed]~~ run
~~tire~~ tire tracks across your
back ~~[crossed]~~ I can see you
had your fun. But Darling
can't you see my signals turn from
green to red - I can see a traffic
Jam with you just ~~up~~ ahead

Crosstown Traffic

Crosstown Traffic

~~This piece A little advice my friend you just quit~~
    I know that I'm not just
the only one you try - to
hitch up on a ride. those
tire marks on your back
and even a few scooter
tracks ~~show me~~ you ~~didn't~~
~~just get~~ from just sleeping
on the road side
    Shows me I aint
the only

More than just a guitar wizard, Jimi Hendrix was also a songwriter of lasting influence—and conscious craft,
as these two rough drafts illustrate.

Purple Haze
— Jesus Saves

Purple Haze...Beyond insane
Is it pleasure or is it
Pain —
Down On the ~~ceiling~~ ceiling
lookeing up ~~at~~ at The
Bed... See my Body painted
Blue and red —

     I see fetus unborns
~~Why is everybody~~
pointing at the Time ---
Rush through space...
My Hair is Blowing in thier minds
~~Faster~~ through the Haze
I see 1,000 crosses
Scratched in the

"NEVER MY LOVE"

D & D

YOU ASK ME IF THERE'LL COME A TIME
WHEN I GROW TIRED OF YOU
NEVER MY LOVE
REPEAT

YOU WONDER IF THIS HEART OF MINE
WILL LOSE ITS DESIRE FOR YOU
NEVER MY LOVE
REPEAT ?

WHAT MAKE YOU THINK LOVE WILL END
WHEN YOU KNOW THAT MY WHOLE LIFE DEPENDS
REPEAT DEPENDS — ON YOU

VERSE YOU SAY YOU FEAR I'LL CHANGE MY MIND
I WON'T REQUIRE YOU
NEVER MY LOVE   REPEAT (NEVER MY LOVE)

BA BA BA BA (VERSE MELODY)
HOW CAN YOU (THINK) LOVE WILL END
WHEN I'VE ASKED YOU TO SPEND
YOU'RE WHOLE LIFE
WITH ME

NEVER MY LOVE NEVER MY LOVE
BIG NEVER MY LOVE.

One night in 1967, Richard Addrisi's brother, Don, proposed to his girlfriend. "Will there ever come a time when you grow tired of me?" she asked. He looked into her eyes and said, "Never, my love." He drove home, awakened his brother, and told him he had a great idea for a song. As cowriter Richard recalled, "I set a cup of coffee down on the rough draft and it made a ring. My mother had some bacon on a paper towel, and she slapped it down on top of the song: "Here, eat. You've got to put something in your stomach when you're writing." And I remember turning around and saying: "Mom, this is our hit song!"

SUGAR MAGNOLIA BLOSSOMS BLOOMIN
HEADS ALL EMPTY & I DONT CARE
SAW MY BBY DOWN BY TH RIVER
KNEW SHE'D HAVE TO COME UP SOON FOR AIR

SWEET BLOSSOM COME ON UNDER THE WILLOW
WE CAN HAVE HIGH TIMES IF YOU'LL ABIDE
WE CAN DISCOVER THE WONDERS OF NATURE
ROLLIN IN THE RUSHES DOWN BY THE RIVER

SHE'S GOT EVERYTHING DELIGHTFUL
SHE'S '' '' I NEED
TAKES THE WHEEL WHEN I'M SEEIN DOUBLE
PAYS MY TICKETS WHEN I SPEED

SOMETIME WHEN THE CUCKOO'S CRYIN
WHEN THE MOON IS HALFWAY DOWN
SOMETIME WHEN THE NITE IS DYING
TAKE ME OUT & WANDER ROUND   PAE DA EBAE

SHE COMES SKIMMING THROUGH RAYS OF VIOLET
SHE CAN WADE IN A DROP OF DEW
SHE DONT COME AND I DONT FOLLOW
WAITS BACK STAGE WHILE I SING TO YOU

SHE CAN DANCE A CAJUN RHYTHM
JUMP LIKE A WILLYS IN 4 WHEEL DRIVE
SHES A SUMMER LOVE IN THE SPRING FALL & WINTER
SHE CAN MAKE HAPPY ANY MAN ALIVE

    S   G   E   D
    S   G   E   IN
A BREEZE IN THE PINES IN THE SUMER NITE MAS
CRAZY IN THE SUNLITE YES INDEED

Classic songs from two great—but very different—sixties bands: "Never My Love" by the Association and the Grateful Dead's "Sugar Magnolia."

God is a concept by which we measure our pain

I'll say it again

God is a concept by which we measure our pain

I don't believe in MAGIC

I don't believe in I CHING

I don't believe in BIBLE

I don't believe in TAROT

"   "   "   HITLER

"   "   "   JESUS

"   "   "   KENNEDY

"   "   "   BUDDHA

"   "   "   MANTRA

"   "   "   GITA

"   "   "   YOGA

"   "   "   KINGS

"   "   "   ELVIS

"   "   "   ZIMMERMAN

"   "   "   BEATLES

I just believe in me   But   WOW   I'm John
Yoko and me   And so dear friends
And that's reality.   You'll just have to carry
The dream is over   on
What can I say?   The dream is over.
The dream is over
Yesterday
I was the dream weaver
But now I'm reborn
I was the walrus

Two songwriting icons at work: John Lennon and Bob Dylan.

slinding inside my grave ʲ . . . . . . ʲ . . . . . . ˡʳˢ ʲᵘᵉ,ᵛ ᶠᵍᵒᵒ ᵍᵏᶠ
˙ ʳᵏᵈʲᶠʰ

gtng dwn to trate pnts

fix all these womn brokn hearts to run

G H:IERTMAJU FJSQ HA CJS FGT   DJDJFK

:::FKGJTIGJKLFKGJVVV,BMBMV,V,

YOU CANT GET YOUR WAY ALLA TIME

   DLFKRIT ...and now you ...(?) whilemi remain here

____
   farmer's daugter   I'd go all the way with you but...
when the dawn comes, i am not alone anymore

when the nite comes, i have(not0 my freedom to disappear
         robbedp me of my grave
           burler's tools
                         vibrate
   plauge   chemicals ..lazy afternoon
     up is up & gone is gone   i'm sitting here here thinking
____   after doing drinking...etc
        mam aclosed the
              door on the suna
        PLEDGING MY TIME if nothing comes outa this, you'll soon
                         know

____

mam youre so hard...guilty for just being there
                    (or else-man feel down-"song"
                "lost in foundalk in terms of what if x8the av.

       (,...youre so hard) man in drag
                      helpless like rich man's child
       last

WHITE LOVE &....song

YELLOW MONDAY... SONG

i did it so you wouldnt have to (do it) SONG

1. corss fire 2. hey baby 3. jullieta 4. you go your way, i'll go
                                         mine
       5. love will endire
            6. little baby

NOBODY'S ....ETCX...SoNG

well they dl know my fate
(river boat captn)
have to wait

well i dont know how it happened
but the riverboat captain — he knows my fate
but everybody else / even yourself is just gonna
have to wait

PART THREE

Peaceful Feelings

(Archive Photos)

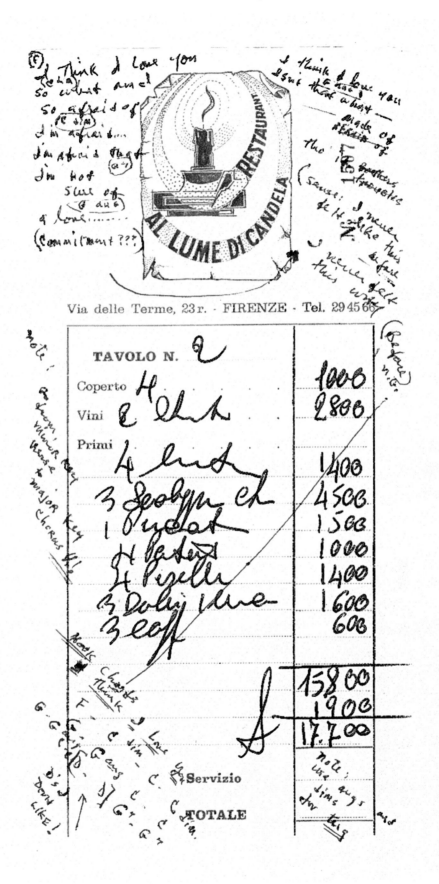

One of the original working pages — or, more accurately, receipts — for David Cassidy's "I Think I Love You."

I Think I Love You

DAVID CASSIDY

Songwriter Tony Romeo contributed David Cassidy's breakout hit.

How did you first hear about the TV show?

The Partridge Family was to have been *The Cowsills.* It was going to be their story, their group, with their mother in it and all. And by that time they had gotten pretty big, and they couldn't really come to an agreement, and so it was decided, okay, we'll create our own. So they had an open call for about a hundred Screen Gems writers to watch the pilot for this thing. And it seems to me that every one of us just looked at each other when we left the screening room on Fifth Avenue and thought, "Oh, God, nobody's going to touch this!" and then we all went home to write for it. What a bunch of whores. At that time, I had been working on this real dirgey, minor-key song that started in C minor and then went to G and then to [G]7, and it was going to be so poignant and heartbreaking—and then, when I

made the connection to pitch this for the Partridges, I made it real zany. I will also tell you that the single was sickening to me. I detested it, I hated it. When I heard it, I thought, "What? All you have to do is stick with the demo!" I prayed for its demise. I really did.

Is this how you wrote a lot of songs back then—just go from one piece of paper to the next?

Listen, envelopes from bills are not safe! The only things that are spared are things I'd need for the IRS. I'll go digging through files today for something like an old bank statement, and I'll look on the back of it and find something written there.

What about those notes on the side, though? "Keep it this way," you wrote to yourself.

Yeah, I was trying to guide myself, because I knew it was going to be a long haul. That's the only way I would be able to frame the long lines; they were real long. Because by the time I descend . . . and then "I think I love you"—that's a long haul, and I have to pick it up to keep some interest until I get to that title. To me, it just seemed a little too rambly, so that's why I made the notation about "cartoon," to make it a little frantic.

Part of the rough is on an Italian-language receipt. Did you start writing before you went to Italy, or start it there and come back to finish it?

I had the original idea, and then I'd gone to Italy to scribble around with it, because I'm always working with songs. When I came back, I started to hone it for *The Partridge Family.*

So you worked on it here, then in Italy, then here again. That's a lot of dedication.

No, it wasn't just for that song; it's like, that was my life, you know. I was a songwriter.

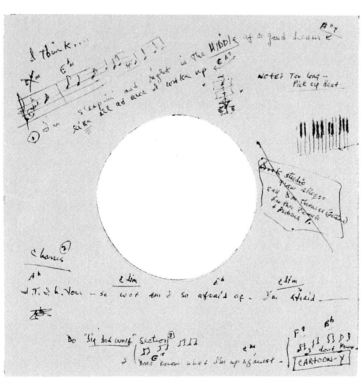

I'm sleepin' in the middle of a good dream
and right in the middle of
"...likeness..." At once I woke up
from something that keeps knockin' at my brain [head]
before I go insane I hold my pillow to my head
and spring up in my bed
screaming out, the words I dread   I think I love you!!!

(Repeat verse) - "talk about it
"go and shout it"

Go to Chorus:
(F)
I think I love you
C dim
So what am I so afraid of (F)
C dim
I'm afraid that
I'm not sure of
a love there is no cure for

Sure of
cure for

Ain't that what life is made of?
AMBIVALENCE
titles: this old ??? ???

- Call Wes.
- Meet G. at JFK
Flt. 16 Braniff
3:20 am
- Call Allegra
May 1 - 9:15 am
↓
Emily Februsins.
Tex-Mex Bash
25'd - 1356
↓
Call Susanna du Plant
Gilbert Adv.
PL 2 - 8833

Raindrops Keep Falling on My Head

**B. J.
THOMAS**

Stephen Bishop interviewed Oscar-winning songwriters Hal David and Burt Bacharach.

This looks like an early, early lyric.

HD: Well, I only wrote three drafts; this one wasn't my first and it wasn't the last, so it must be the one in the middle.

Did you and Burt Bacharach have B. J. Thomas in mind as you were writing it?

HD: Not initially. We thought of Ray Stevens, we thought of Arlo Guthrie, but we went to B. J. Thomas because we knew he was a great singer. We were familiar with him from Scepter Records, where we had Dionne Warwick, so we knew how he sang and how good he was. It was a good choice.

Did you actually see the sequence in the movie Butch Cassidy {and the Sundance Kid} that you wrote the song for?

HD: Oh, yeah. We saw it before we actually signed to do the movie. We wrote the song for the sequence.

Did you already have the idea "raindrops keep falling on my head"?

HD: No. It came from the sequence and the music.

How is the business different now from the way it was then?

HD: Well, now the business is largely controlled by the artist-writer, the singer-writer, the writer-singer. In the old days there were very few people who were writers *and* singers. For professional writers, it used to be that if you had the right song you had all the artists in the world at your fingertips. We don't quite have it that way anymore.

When you were working with Hal David, would you sing mumbo-jumbo lyrics to him to convey the melody?

BB: Sometimes, but sometimes it would be something that would stick and work, like "Raindrops." That's a title I kept singing when I was writing it.

Oh, so you already had the title?

BB: He wanted to change it, to get something else. But he kept coming back to it. I guess sometimes it just feels good. It just drops out of the sky.

At first, was there anything funny about doing a contemporary song for a period-piece Western movie?

BB: No, I just felt that wasn't a hard boundary to cross. A picture in the twenties would be a different thing; this movie was long ago, but it could have been now or then, you know.

It added to the fun of the scene.

BB: It was a look into [Paul] Newman's character. It was dangerous to do something like that in the middle of a picture; I didn't have any doubt about it working, but I'm sure the filmmakers did.

That {song} was nominated, wasn't it?

BB: It won. Yeah, score did, too. Good year. . . .

Raindrops Keep Fallin On My Head
But I'm not the kind of guy who
likes to stay in bed
So I'm gettin' wet - those
Raindrops will make the flowers grow
While they're growin - I'm Gonna

Pick me a rose for my lapel
Then I'll throw a penny in the nearest
wishin well
Wishin is for me - ~~these~~
Raindrops are Fallin On My Head
~~They~~ keep fallin - But I don't

Care not me
As loud as it may thunder
I won't thunder
I never ~~and I don't~~ need a big umbrella
to walk under

Raindrops keep Walkin On My Head
But that doesn't mean my eyes
will soon be turnin' red
Cryin's not for me - Cause
I'm Keepin' busy as a bee being happy
It's a Wonderful life
Such a Wonderful life
(This is the life + its ~~good~~ good life)

We've Only Just Begun

THE CARPENTERS

Songwriter and actor Paul Williams got his big break with the Carpenters' hit.

When did you start dabbling in writing?

I sat at home watching daytime television, and that got really boring; I was waiting for the phone to ring as an actor, and it didn't. I started dabbling in guitar a little bit. I couldn't play other people's songs, so I started doodling, you know, writing my own. I wrote multi-verse, boring protest songs, and one guy signed me to a lifelong career as a writer and singer and recording artist. After about five weeks they let me go, said they didn't think I had a future in music.

And then you went to A&M Records?

I went into A&M, and they were looking for a lyricist for this guy named Roger Nichols, and Roger and I started writing together. We had tons of album cuts. It seemed like we were never going to hear anything of ours on the radio—until Three Dog Night recorded a song called "Out in the Country," which made it to the Top Ten. At the same time, we wrote a bank commercial. Crocker Bank was going to do a commercial showing a young couple getting married, kissing, and at the reception, then riding off into the sunset. It was going to say, "You have a long way to go. We'd like to help you get there. The Crocker Bank."

And that was "We've Only Just Begun."

Roger and I wrote this commercial. I sang it, and we were in mixing a demo of something else, and I grabbed an envelope and scratched down those lyrics, and it was probably the record that changed our lives.

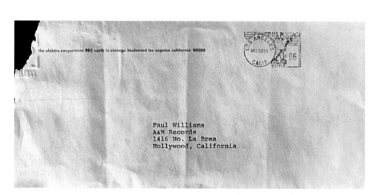

The other side of the fated envelope.

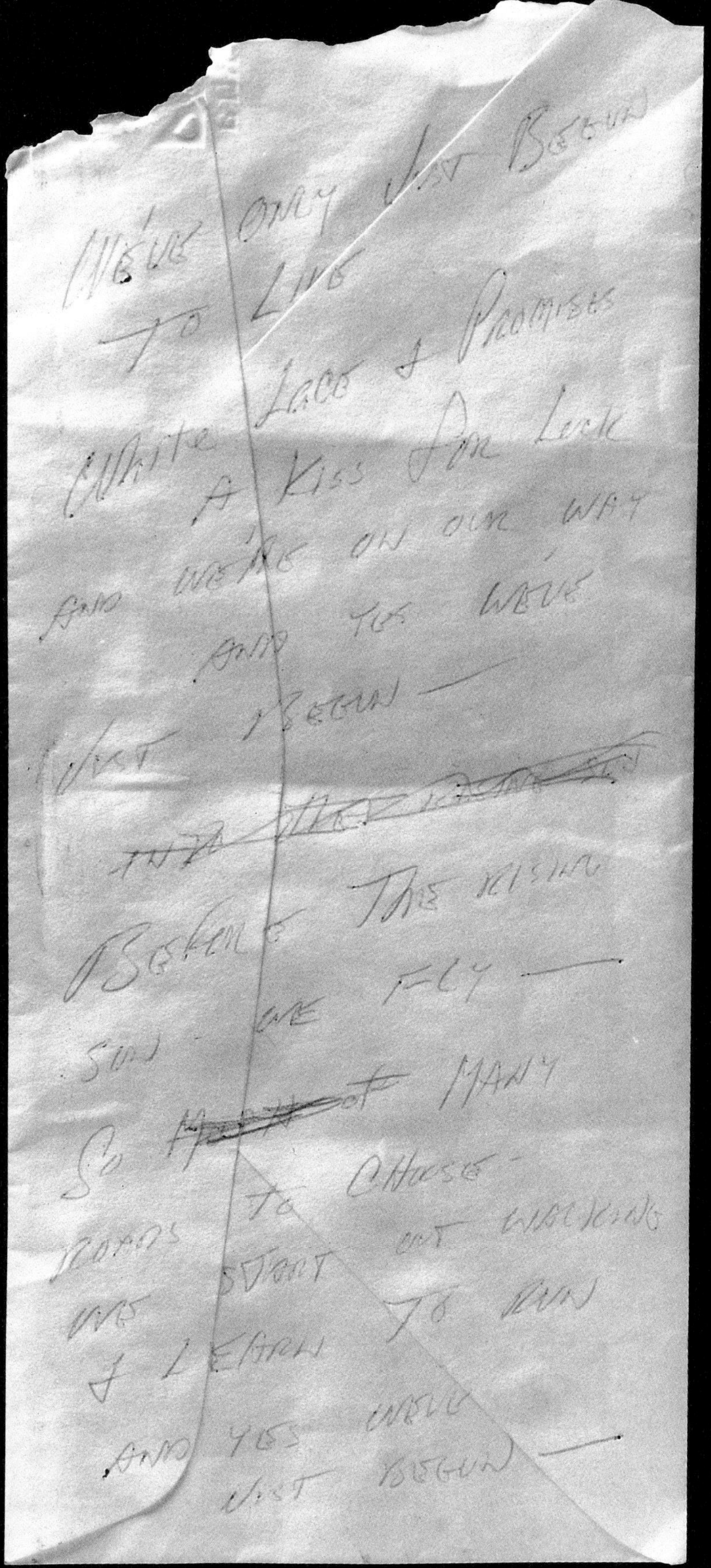

WE'VE ONLY JUST BEGUN
TO LIVE

WHITE LACE & PROMISES
A KISS FOR LUCK
AND WE'RE ON OUR WAY
AND YES, WE'VE
BEGUN —

~~JUST~~
~~AND AFTER~~

BEFORE THE RISING
SUN WE FLY —

SO ~~MANY~~ MANY
ROADS TO CHOOSE
WE START OUT WALKING
& LEARN TO RUN
AND YES WE'VE
JUST BEGUN —

I WANA JAM it with You
HoPe You LiKe Jamming Too
Do it ANY How
I ANd I will See You
THROUGH

EVery DAY we PAy the Price LiVie SACRIFICE
JAMMING till The JAM is
through

SAM ine
JAm it in The name of the Lord
Jamming straight from 'yard.

Two rough drafts from very different worlds: Bob Marley's "Jammin'" and Elton John's "Levon."

Levon:

Levon wears his war wound like a crown
he calls his child Jesus,
cause he likes the name
and he sends him to the finest school in town.
Levon
Levon, likes his money
he makes alot they say
spends his days counting ~~money~~
in a garage by the ~~side of the~~ waterway.

RPT
*
He was born a pauper to a pawn
on a christmas day, when the New York times
said God is dead, and the war begun
and Alvin Tostig has a son, today

RPT
and
1 And he shall be Levon
2 he shall be a good man
3 a simply splendid citizen
4 in tradition with ~~the~~ family plan.

*
Levon sells cartoon baloons in town
his family business ~~thrives~~
Jesus blows up baloons all day.
Sits on the porch swing watching them fly.
and Jesus
He wants to go to venus
leave Levon ~~far~~ behind
take a baloon and go sailing
                   levon
while Levon slowly dies.

* RPT.
2 RPT
    3 RPT
* 1 he shall be Levon
    2
③ 1

"Levon"
-Elton John
Bernie Taupin

You Don't Mess Around with Jim

JIM
CROCE

Jim Croce's widow, Ingrid, remembers her beloved husband.

I didn't realize it, but you and your husband were a duo at first. When did you start singing together?

From the time we met. That's how we met. He was a judge in a contest I was performing for, in Philadelphia. I had just turned sixteen and Jim was twenty or twenty-one.

How did he write back then?

It usually all came out at once. He'd have some kinds of books around. He was an avid reader. He would read two or three books a day sometimes. He really tried to hide the fact that he was as bright as he was, because he didn't want to intimidate people from talking to him or make them feel uncomfortable around him. So he used to talk with more of a dialect than he really had; when I met him he sounded like a college professor. And as time moved on and he changed out of three-piece suits into work clothes and relaxing with life, he changed his attitude, and his songs started to take on a more traditional flavor. And I think that's why they've been around so long—the sources he drew from initially were very traditional American music. I wouldn't call it folk music or rock or even light rock. We call it jazz and rhythm and blues. It's really storytelling material.

Jim had started writing from the time he was young. He would change or add words to things, you know, like when he'd hear songs that he'd only get a part of, he'd make up stuff and kind of finish them off. He was influenced by Fats Waller, Jimmie Rodgers, a lot of blues, and I'd say Sinatra in terms of phrasing. And also Woody Guthrie was a big influence on Jim. Jim was really an historian; his father used to have wonderful 78s that he'd play all the time. Music was a big

part of their family. He'd performed since he was a little boy, at church functions and things of that sort.

So he started at a very young age. Playing the accordion, right?

Yeah—five, I think, five or six. I think he got his first guitar when he was about seventeen. He was working at a hospital, and this guy that was doing construction work across the street had a guitar that he used to play at lunch hour, and Jim got really excited about it. He played mostly country guitar and bluegrass. He ended up being one of Jim's heroes—his name was Jim Reed. Jim said, "Oh, I've got to get a guitar," and he said, "Well, I'll teach you how to play the guitar if you get one." So he and his dad went out to a pawn shop and I think they traded in one of his brother's old clarinets or something for a guitar.

Who was "Jim" in "You Don't Mess Around with Jim"?

"Jim" was a lot of people. Jim Croce was a lot of people, but the songs were a lot of people. They were not all about one person. They were all eclectic. They come from different periods of time. What Jim would do when he talked to people is bring out who they were, so they became a part of him. All these characters became a part of Jim's personality, or at least the personality who wrote the music.

This is obviously a really rough draft—it's really just a sheet covered with figures, but with a little bit of rough writing that's the germ of the song. Now this is your writing, here, where it says "rent, electric" . . .

Probably. If it has to do with numbers, it's me. Yeah, because if it has anything to do with dollars . . . We never had any money. When Jim died, he had one shirt and a pair of pants.

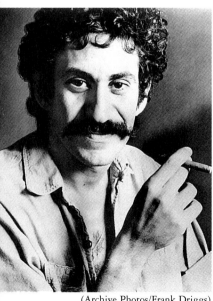

(Archive Photos/Frank Driggs)

yea Big Jim got listed
he finally fund out where it at
sure aint no hustlin people you dont
kno

even if you do got a custom made
2 piece pool cue $53.00
                        25   75.

        25
         5
         5
    20.00 $40.00
     5.00   175   100.00 75.00
    22.00   50.00 52.00
     5.00   23.00
    52.00 $190.00 100.00
   125.00   25   180.00
    75.00   65.00
   152.00   Rent 125.00
                            65.00
                            6.00
             $5.00
             20.00   Electri

You Dont
Mess Around   9.08   15.0   175.00
With Jim   52.00
                          5   23.0
             70   5
                         50

Peaceful Easy Feeling

(Henry Diltz)

*J*ack Tempchin wrote the early Eagles hit.

How old were you when you started writing songs?

I didn't start playing until I was almost twenty. I was out of high school. I'd started playing harmonica when I was about seventeen.

Did you meet Longbranch Pennywhistle—Glenn Frey, J. D. Souther—way back then?

I actually met them at the Candy Company when I was in college. They were playing; they were going to stay with some people, and I offered to let them stay at my house. At the time, I had a big house in the hippie area, so I had my brother and six guys living there, and a candle shop in the garage. So every time J. D. and Glenn came down to San Diego, they would stay at my house.

Tell me where you were when you wrote "Peaceful Easy Feeling," why you wrote it. The rough draft is on the back of a flyer for the Jack Tempchin Revue.

Yeah, that's all connected with it. This friend of mine had made this poster for me when I was playing at the Candy Company. This poster found its way out to El Centro somehow, and there was a guy out there who had a coffeehouse and he hired me to play there. I'd never been out there before, but I met this girl there—and nothing happened, but it's a real desert out there, and that's where I wrote most of "Peaceful Easy Feeling."

Was it about the girl?

Kinda, but really only sorta about her. Then I got back to town, and I was working on it and went down to the street fair and I saw this other girl. She was Mexican and had these silver earrings, so I just put her in there, too. I was just thinking about girls twenty-four hours a day at that time. I used to just walk around with my Stella guitar, which I bought for thirteen dollars at a pawn shop; it was my first guitar. And I was at a Wiener schnitzel and had ordered something, and I was in the parking lot waiting, and that's when I wrote the last verse. So that's the story—I don't remember much more than that, it was so long ago.

You obviously wrote it on guitar.

Yeah, finger-picked it in E.

It's such a classic song. I think it'll be played many years from now.

Man, I hope so. You know how it is—you just write all these songs and people look at them and go, "What an oddball you are." Others, they say, "This is great." There's no way of knowing beforehand.

PAINT $6.00

Electric wiring $7.20

Heater $3.00

It makes me smile and makes me sing
And kiss You all up and down clothes
I'm just Livin' Like a Natural man Letters
I feel my Love tumblin' rollin down

I AIN'T gonna Let You down

Baby I'll do the best for You I can

MY head is clear and I'm feelin so good

Its somethin that I just don't understan

It's a peaceful easy feeling

I found out a long time ago
The way a woman can get to affect Your soul
But she can't take You anywhere (here)
That Your not ready to go
can't take You anywhere that You Don't already
know how to go.

(I got To go You got To stay

work out fine

I got feelin for everyone
Let my Light shine

I Like the way Your sparkln
earrings swing
Against Your skin so brown
I wanta sleep with You in
The desert night
with a billion stars all
around

Best of My Love/Heartache Tonight

THE EAGLES

J.D. Souther, good friend of the Eagles (and of Stephen Bishop), wrote two of their biggest hits.

So when did you start writing? C'mon, play along! Don't make this hard on me. This is tough to do with someone you already know.

I never wrote a song until I was twenty-one. When I first came to California from Texas, I was just singing and playing drums. I started writing because some of the guys in my band were writing songs on an acoustic guitar, and they had little publishing deals. I thought they were not very good songs, and I figured if they could get, you know, fifty dollars a week, whatever they were getting for writing these really mediocre songs, that I could probably do it, too.

So you started writing, and you played with Glenn Frey, and you would write a little with him. How come they didn't ask you to join the Eagles?

Well, we rehearsed one afternoon at the Troubador together, but we just kind of looked at each other and went, "This isn't what any of us want." I didn't want to be in a band. Glenn wanted a band. That's why we broke up. He wanted to make the band bigger. I wanted to play songs by myself. So I guess we both got what we wanted.

Was "Best of My Love" just you and Glenn?

Nope, Don [Henley], too. They were actually in London working on an album. I talked to them on the phone from Peter Asher's house.

Who came up with the title?

I think Glenn, but I'm not sure. It wasn't me. I know he had the little guitar riff that's in the beginning, this little C-tuning thing he has. And we were talking on the phone and he said, "We got this thing and it needs a bridge."

Back then, you would just put it on cassette, take it back, work on it later. . . .

Mostly we just sat in a room with a guitar and a bunch of legal tablets and just played it until it was finished. There's a certain amount of everybody going to their corners and coming back the next day with whatever ideas they might have had.

I always thought that when you write with someone, you've got to have moments of silence. If everyone's always talking or if everyone's trying to come up with something, you can't really concentrate. So how did you get together with all of these people to write "Heartache Tonight"? You guys sat down and . . .

We didn't do it sitting down! We did it, actually, walking around my living room. We were walking around just clapping, {sings} "Somebody's gonna hurt someone," just the way the record's made. No instruments; we just started singing it.

Where did Bob Seger fit in?

I can't remember whether he had the chorus first or not. But he was in Detroit. We weren't working on it at the same time. He was on the phone with Glenn and Don about it. Bob wrote the chorus and we wrote the rest of the song. Bob thought of the title. {looking at the rough draft} Yeah, this is mostly my writing, which is incredibly verbose and endless. The whole trick for me is to cut back. I write nine pages and maybe there's a page of good lyrics in it.

So you've collaborated a lot; you've written songs on your own. Seems like you like collaborating better.

No, actually, I like writing by myself better. Collaborating serves the highest purpose of all for me, though, which is to finish the song.

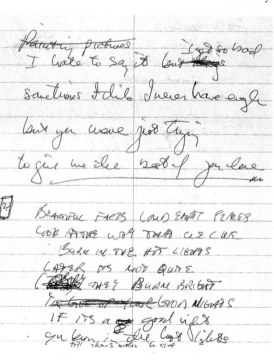

"BEST OF MY LOVE"

I could see it was ~~driving crazy~~ ...

~~But I...~~

Somehow the words came out too ~~rough~~

Here in my heart...

~~For a long time~~

Going back in time I was ~~...~~ her face

and I wished the same for you

~~...~~

As like a day you see

and when you look at me

I think that all those eyes

are staring through

Every morning I wake up at morning

what's your upper ...

The Shuffle

Somebody's gonna hurt someone
  before the night is through
Somebody's gonna come undone
  might as well be you

(1)

Everybody wants to touch somebody
  touch 'em good and hot
Everybody wants to take a little chance
  maybe love, maybe not
There's gonna be a heartache tonight
  heartache tonight, I know
Gonna be a heartache tonight
  heartache tonight   I know

~~Its~~ ~~any kinda~~ ~~fun~~ just to ship around ~~~~
~~Anybody~~ ~~~~ on the loose ~~~~
...... Hot Summer nights

Radio unless you wanna drive to town
  and ~~hope~~ it comes out right

Some people like to stay out late
  Some begin to fade
But nobody wants to go home now
its still dark and your plans ain't made

A HEARTACHE TONIGHT

(5)

    G   Em

Somebody's gonna hurt somebody
before the night is through
somebody's gonna come undone
* might as well be you

Everybody wants to hold somebody
it takes all night
and Everybody wants to take a little chance
and make it come out right

there's gonna be a heartache tonight
a heartache tonight I know
there's gonna be a heartache tonight
a heartache tonight

    A   D

⟵ ~~Some people~~ like to stay out late
~~Nobody~~ wants to have no one
* would ya like to have a place to go
days speed all night long
⟵ Nobody wants to go home now
Summer nights are gonna stay till dawn
(Stay out and make love 'til dawn)
~~Some people like to shop~~
~~   ~~ around
to see what they can get
Nobody wants to go home now
Music's playin and we ain't done yet

She's Gone

Stephen Bishop interviewed Daryl Hall.

In your writing, it sounds like you're a title man. It sounds like you come up with the title, and then write the song.

I almost always start with a title. In fact, what seems to have developed over the years is I'll get a groove or some kind of a chord pattern, and the title will come. Sometimes the title will come first, and then after that I start piecing the verses together. But it almost always stems from the central title idea.

So what were you like in high school? Did you know John {Oates} back then?

I met John when I was a senior in high school, in Philadelphia. I had a street-corner group called The Temp-Tones, and he was in a band called The Masters, and we met at a battle of the R&B bands.

Did either of you win?

Not that one. Actually, let me think—that wasn't a talent show. We were actually promoting our singles. He had a single on a small label, and I had a single also with Gamble and Huff, and we were supposed to get up and lip-sync our records. And a big fight broke out—shots and all. That's how we met.

"She's Gone" was early on.

That was one of the first songs John and I wrote together. John had come up with the chord pattern on acoustic guitar. When I first heard it, I thought it sounded like a Cat Stevens song. He was playing this pattern and kind of mumbling something, and I sat down at the piano, and the way I played it was the way you heard it on the record. It sort of changed the song, gave it more of a soul feel, more R&B. He was singing that low melody, and then I started the octave above him because I didn't know what else to do. I didn't want to sing a harmony part, so that's how that happened. Then we pooled our experiences: He was breaking up with a girlfriend, and I was breaking up with my wife at the time, so we just sort of pooled what was going on in our lives. The lyrics came really fast. I think we wrote the lyrics in about a half hour.

I can't even keep track of all your hits. Is there a hit formula?

I never found one. I just went with what I thought were my strengths over the years. I always came up with melodies pretty easily. Really no formula, though. I always wrote from honesty; still do, from real situations or observations. There's no real set way to do it.

What about technical tricks?

I always have a tape recorder on, because I can never remember what I do after I do it. So if anything is brewing, I immediately push the button on the tape deck. These days, I try to work close to some kind of drum machine, because grooves tend to stimulate me. Not always, but I'll sit and start playing chords to the groove or the drum pattern, or sometimes I'll come up with a chord pattern first. It depends on the song. Then I'll start singing a melody over whatever I've started playing.

(Archive Photos)

She's Gone

~~everybodys tryin to~~   on consolation
everybodies high ~~tonite on comfort~~
~~everne is~~
everybodies tryin to tell me what is right for m
my daddy tried to bore me w/ a ~~bother~~ sermon
but its plain to see that they cant comfort me

sorry charlie for the imposition
I think ~~I got it t~~ ~~got~~ got the strength to carry on
~~give me~~ a drink and a quick decision
I need
        oh ~~now~~ its up to me ~~me~~ what will be

and shes gone gone gone — ~~to~~ I pray
2   you better learn how to face it
1   ~~spot~~ pay the devil to replace her

        shes gone . . . . what went wrong
got up in the ~~mirror~~ morning look in the mirror
(Im) worn as her toothbrush hanging in the stand
my face aint lookin any younger
oh I can see loves taken her toll on me
                chor

most verse

Oh — LAS VEGAS

1st time I lose I drink whiskey
2nd time I lose I drink gin
3rd " " " drink most anything
cause I know I gonna win.

[Remember "Night People"]

(spades)

① Queen o' hearts is a friend
o' mine ——— + th' Quee
o' Hearts is a Bitch +
Some day ~~when I make my mind~~ ~~up my~~
mind up. — I'll find ~~out~~ what
is wild (or) I'll know 'cause
I'll get Rich.]
~~But the day without~~ when I don't care
~~cause I know I gonna be~~ broke

In the 1970s, pioneer country rocker Gram Parsons joined Hank Williams and Buddy Holly in honky-tonk heaven.
This is the rough draft of his classic, "Ooh Las Vegas."

(B) Ooh-Las Vegas — ...
'Please don't drag me
Down Beneath your
Marble ~~Hilton~~ floor — I said Ooh
Las Vegas — ~~(###)~~ Not
first time ~~the~~ that your
Bounced ~~to~~ me but your
'door — ~~that no water~~
~~~~ &I know you
[~~########~~→think that !!m a
loser — ~~#######~~ But I don't care
looking you 'll cause
come back — Begging for
some more!

The Way We Were

BARBRA STREISAND

Alan and Marilyn Bergman wrote the Oscar-winning No. 1 hit.

When you were growing up, what influences did you have in learning how to write? Did it come from writing poetry in high school?

AB: Well, I did. We always read a lot. That's one thing. We were also very lucky in that we had mentors. Marilyn and I had a wonderful mentor/lyric writer by the name of Bob Russell, and I had Johnny Mercer and Leo Robbin. They listened to everything I wrote, criticized, helped that way.

Early influences?

MB: I loved the Fred Astaire and Ginger Rogers movies, for example. When I was a kid, the Hollywood musicals, Judy Garland, Gene Kelly, Fred Astaire, they were all in their heyday. Now, looking back, you realize that that's some of the greatest literature in popular music. Irving Berlin and George Gershwin and Harold Arlen and Jerome Kern. The first time I ever went to the musical theater was to see *Oklahoma,* and I remember it just blew my mind.

AB: I remember the first piece of sheet music I ever bought. It was by Johnny Mercer. You know, the great influences.

So when did you two first meet Barbra {Streisand}?

MB: We first met Barbra in 1962, I believe. She was singing down at the Bon Soir, and Stewey Stein took us down to hear her. I'd never heard anyone like her in my life.

AB: And Marilyn cried.

MB: I like crying. And we've been friends ever since.

MB: I think "The Way We Were" may be the only time we ever got a good title to write a title song to.

AB: In talking about "The Way We Were," I'd like to dispel something, because another person wrote a book about it and he got it all wrong. When we finished the song, we had two or three months before Barbra was going to record it, because the film was still shooting. And Marilyn and I said, "Everyone likes it, but let's see if we could write some other song called 'The Way We Were.'" So Marvin wrote another melody and we wrote another lyric, to function the same way that song worked in the movie—as a corridor back into time. But this lyric was a little more cerebral. And Barbra loved it, Sydney Pollack loved it, so we decided the best way to know which to use was to have Barbra record both of them and lay each of them against the images in the film. And the first one we wrote—which became the big hit—worked with the images, and the other one didn't.

MB: We called it "The Way We Weren't." It's on Barbra's retrospective album.

The Way We Were

{Memories
~~Daydreams~~ light the corners of my mind

Misty watercolor memories
~~faded~~
of the way we were.

~~Scattered~~ Pictures of the smiles we left behind —

Of the time we loved each other

{And the way we were
{For the way we were

{Smiles we gave
~~to~~ one another
Smiles we had
for one another

Can it be that it was ~~all so~~ ~~just and~~ simple then

Or has time rewritten every line?

If we had the chance to do it all again

Tell me would we? could we?
?

Memories may be beautiful and yet

What's too painful to remember

We simply choose to forget
sometimes
often
But/ So it's the laughter we will remember

Whenever we remember

The Way We Were

Only Women Bleed/No More Mr. Nice Guy

ALICE
COOPER

We found "Only Women Bleed" on a record sleeve. Micky Dolenz came over to my house for a party. I showed him the book and he said, "You know what, I think I have something you'd be interested in. I kept this all these years, when Alice did his demos here."

Oh, that's funny—yeah, because he lived right next door and he was always there at that house, with Albert Brooks and Harry Nilsson. When we were writing—I'd been writing with Dick Wagner—I'd be sitting there, and at least one person was always passed out on the couch. Albert used to come in and rehearse in the bathroom; he would come in and make a sandwich, go into the bathroom, come out four or five hours later and say, "Okay, is this funny?" And he'd do an hour of the funniest stuff in the world. Then we'd say, "Sit down now, and listen to this. Is this a good song?"

Who did you write that song with?

I wrote that with Dick Wagner. He and I wrote all those ballads together. I always had the TV on, and he'd be noodling around with the guitar, and I'd be noodling around with lyrics and everything, and somebody said something *like* "Only women bleed," and I know they didn't really say that. And all of a sudden, I said, "What did he say—'only women bleed'?" And Dick says, "I think so," and I said, "Boy, is that good!" And that was one of those songs that just writes itself. It was written in four minutes.

You had great rock songs, but they were also kind of funny.

I always see Alice Cooper as comedy. I never really looked at Alice Cooper as being scary. I always thought, well, you know, he's a villain, of course, but he's funny. With "Only Women Bleed," a lot of people thought I was trying to get away with some kind of . . .

Double entendre?

Yeah, and at the time I didn't know I was writing this feminist anthem. I mean, Tina Turner did it, Etta James did it. It was the one song of mine that was covered by more people than anything else. Women just loved it, because it was a guy singing about women getting the crappy side. They get beat up, always get the bad end of the whole thing. That song was funny, because that was at a time when, no matter where we went, Alice Cooper was the baddest boy in rock 'n' roll. I mean the band. We never did one tenth of the things they said we did. It was like the Sex Pistols, you know—all we had to do was show up and there were twenty-five new rumors.

I remember some of that.

So I said, okay, after all this bad publicity, we're taking the gloves off now—no more Mr. Nice Guy, now we're going to get rough. And it was such a funny song, you know, one of the funniest we ever wrote.

How did you get started?

I was in a band—high school guys—called The Spiders. And we were the local heroes in Phoenix, and we did all Yardbirds and Rolling Stones stuff. We went to L.A. and they ran us out on a rail because everybody was hippies and we were the band that drove the stake through the heart of the love generation.

Was Alice Cooper originally the name of the band or you?

That was the name of the band, but being the front man, I just said, well, I'll be Alice. There were so many rock heroes, so I said, "Let's create the older-than-rock villain." You know, we still talk about him in the third person.

How would you say the business has changed in the past twenty years?

I can't tell. I don't think music has changed that much at all. I don't think what Nirvana does is anything new. I hear a lot of seventies rock, just different versions of it. And all these heavy metal guys are opera singers. I keep wondering, if the guy's going to sing about that, why doesn't he sing with some guts in his throat, you know? I listen to some of it and it's so boring . . .

And you've got to have melody, even if it's heavy heavy metal.

I absolutely agree with you. I mean, I am a Laura Nyro fan. I am a Burt Bacharach fan.

Wow, that's funny. No one would think you'd be a Burt Bacharach fan.

I know every song Burt Bacharach wrote. I used to go to Vegas to see him play. I'd go, "Man, now this guy's a writer."

So when you're bopping around Vegas, are you wearing the leathers and the look?

Not really. I don't go out of my way to be "Here's Alice!" I get recognized enough without it.

But on your credit card it says . . . ?

It says Alice Cooper, yeah.

(Archive Photos)

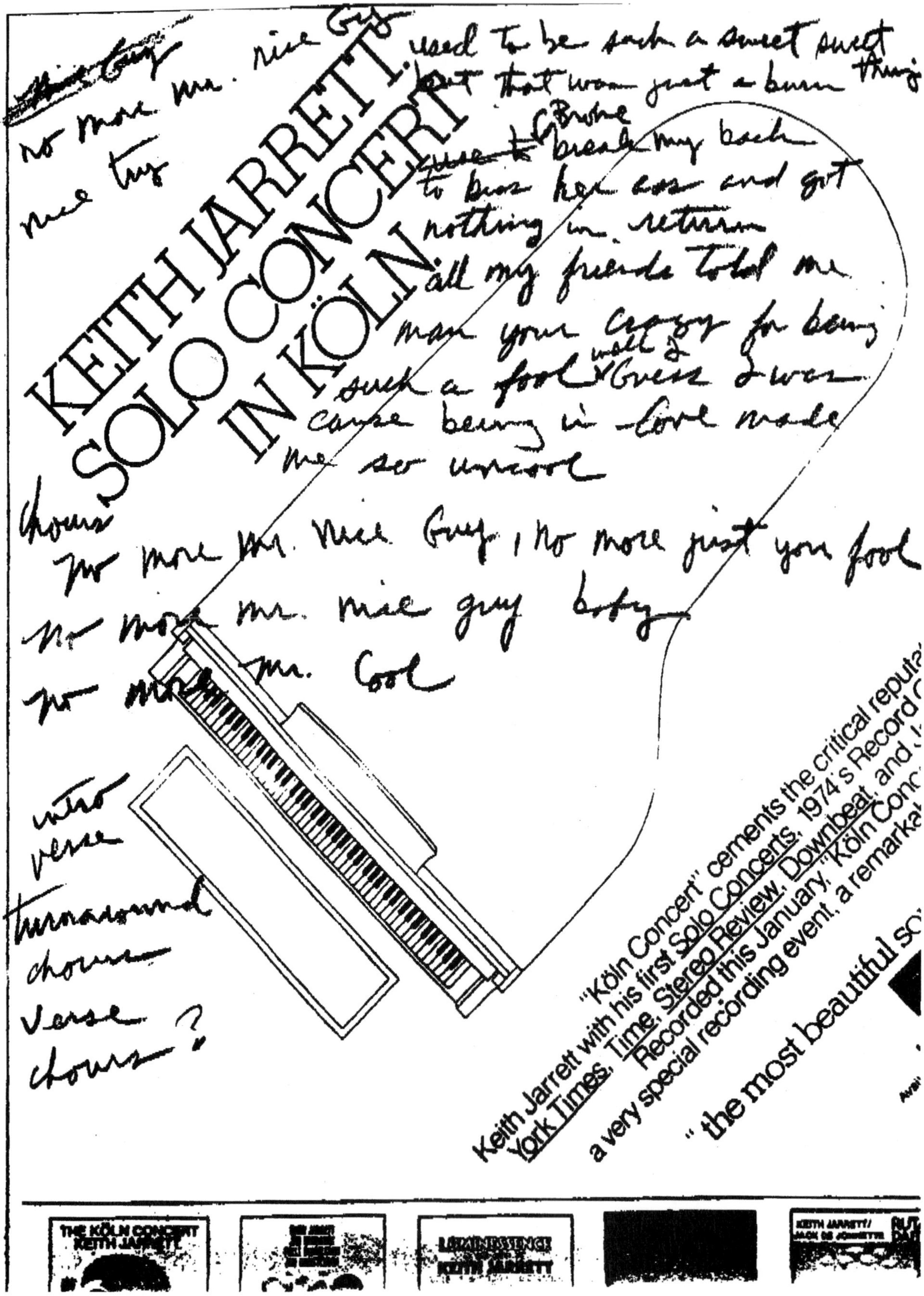

~~Nice Guy~~
no more mr. nice Guy
nice Guy

used to be such a sweet sweet thing
but that was just a burn
~~used to~~ Broke break my back
to kiss her ass and got
nothing in return
all my friends told me
man your crazy for being
such a fool well I Guess I was
cause being in love made
me so uncool

chorus
no more mr. nice Guy, no more just you fool
no more mr. nice guy baby
no more mr. Cool

intro
verse
turnaround
chorus
verse
chorus ?

Rhiannon

FLEETWOOD MAC

(Henry Diltz)

Fleetwood Mac mainstay and successful solo artist Stevie Nicks wrote "Rhiannon."

When you were growing up, what kind of music were your parents playing? What was the first music you remember hearing?

See, my grandad was a country-and-western singer, and a pool player. He really supported himself playing pool, but he looked at himself as a serious singer. I started singing with him when I was about four. The first song we sang was "Are You Mine?," by Red Sovine. Then, when I was in the fourth grade, my grandad knew somebody who had a record store that was going out of business, and he bought all the 45s from that store and brought them to my house in a truck.

Did you start writing poetry when you were really young, or did you pick up a guitar?

A month before I turned sixteen, my mom and dad said I could take guitar lessons. They really didn't know if I was going to like it or not, so they rented me a little guitar, and hired a Spanish classical guitar player, and I took six weeks of guitar lessons, twice a week. And this teacher decided he was going to go to Spain to study, and I loved his guitar so much that they bought it from him for me, for probably a thousand dollars. It was a Goya, a classical guitar; it was very tiny. I still have it. I sat down *that day* and wrote a song. It was pretty goofy, but it had a chorus and two verses and it had an end. And from that second onwards, I knew I wanted to be a songwriter.

Do you remember what it was called?

Okay, it went, "I've loved and I've lost, but I'm sad but not blue/I once loved a boy who was wonderful and true/But he loved another before he loved me/and I knew he still wanted her—'twas easy to see." I truly had fallen, cat's-meow-pajamas, for an incredible guy, and he ended up going out with my best friend. And they both knew I was going to be crushed. I think I've always called it "I've Loved and I've Lost." When I said, "I'm sad but not blue," I was accepting the fact that they were going to be together. I was horrified, but I really loved both of them, and I knew they didn't do it purposefully to hurt me.

Do real romances often work their way into your writing?

Always. I always write, probably my best songs, when they're about a romance. I'll just think about something that happened, and that will take me back to the typewriter and to the piano and guitar. So if I'm really, really happy, I don't write much.

Where did you come up with the name "Rhiannon"?

I got the name from a novel I think I bought in an airport just before a long flight; it was called *Triad,* and it was about a girl named Rhiannon and her sister and mother, or something like that. I just thought the name was so pretty that I wanted to write something about a girl named Rhiannon. I wrote it about three months before I joined Fleetwood Mac, in about 1974. And then to find out that Rhiannon was a real mythical character! I went and read the four books of Rhiannon, and visited the lady who'd translated them. Rhiannon is the maker of birds, and the goddess of steeds; she's the protector of horses. Her music is like a pain pill. When you wake up and hear her birds singing her little song, the danger will have passed. I realized that somehow I had managed to pen a song that went very much along with the mythical tale of Rhiannon. That's when everybody started saying Stevie must be a black witch or something.

Rhiannon rings like a bell thru the night
And wouldn't you love to love her
Takes to the sky like a bird in flight
And who will be her lover

All your life you've never seen
A woman taken to the wind
Would you stay if she promised you heaven
Will you ever win

She is like a cat in the dark
And then she is the darkness
Rules her life like a fine skylark
And when the sky is starless

All your life you've never seen
A woman taken to the wind
Would you stay if she promised you heaven
Will you ever win   Will you ever win
Rhiannon—

she rings like a bell thru the night

Rock and Roll All Night

KISS

(Archive Photos/Fotos Int.)

Gene Simmons—he of the prodigious tongue—wrote the Kiss hit.

When did you actually start writing songs?

I was probably about fourteen. I just started strumming guitar because I loved the Beatles. . . . Then, when I started playing, I couldn't believe that by getting up on stage and playing songs, they'd pay you, and then after they paid you, when you came off, a girl would walk up and say, "So, what are you doing?" So, initially, it was playing other people's songs, and then playing my own tunes. It's very

bizarre—I just finished writing a song called "Seduction of the Innocent," which uses a melody I came up with when I was fourteen, but initially the melody was a kind of middle section for something called "My Girlfriend Gave Me Chocolate Ice Cream."

So you were telling me earlier that "Drive Me Wild" was actually turned into "Rock and Roll All Night."

"Drive Me Wild" was kind of a *Christine*/Stephen King point of view of women. Very sexist, very "you drive me wild, I'll drive you crazy." You know, the girl is a car.

Did you start this off, or was that you and Paul Stanley?

No, I started that on my own, and then the record company said something like, "You have to write a song that tells about your belief in something," and it was Paul who came up with "I want to rock and roll all night and party every day." And then we took "Drive Me Wild," which was that coital pattern that most people know, and the verse, and then together with Paul's chorus we had a song pretty fast. Very Lennon/McCartney that way.

What were the first songs you guys wrote? Do you remember?

You mean actually sitting in a room and strumming chords? Because we've gotten songwriting credit on each other's songs, but we hardly ever sat in the same room. It was very much Lennon/McCartney, you know: McCartney would come in, "Here's a song," and Lennon would say, "The middle eight's no good, how about this?"

(Archive Photos)

KISS - "DRESSED TO KILL"

(I WANNA) ROCK & ROLL All NITE
(STANLEY/SIMMONS)

YOU SHOW US EVERYTHING YOU'VE GOT
YOU KEEP ON DANCING AND THE ROOM GETS HOT
YOU DRIVE US WILD WE'LL DRIVE YOU CRAZY

YOU SAY YOU WANT TO GO FOR A SPIN
THE PARTY'S JUST BEGUN WE'LL LET YOU IN

YOU KEEP A SAYIN' YOU'LL BE MINE FOR AWHILE
YOU'RE LOOKIN' FANCY AND I LIKE YOUR STYLE

YOU SHOW US EVERYTHING YOU'VE GOT
BABY BABY THAT'S QUITE A LOT

I WANNA ROCK AND ROLL ALL NITE
AND PARTY EVERY DAY

"ONCE OVER EASY"
"BURNIN' UP WITH FEVER"

Mamas don't let your ~~baby~~
babies grow up to be cowboys
Don't let 'em pick guitars
and drive ~~pick up trucks~~
them ole trucks —
Make 'em be doctors & lawyers
& such —
Mamas don't let your babies
grow up to be cowboys —
Cuws they'll never stay home
And they're always alone —
Even with someone ~~they~~
love —

A cowboy ain't easy to love & he's harder to hold
He'd rather give you a song than silver or gold -
Budweiser buckles, & soft faded Levi's & each nite
    begins a new day
If you can't understand him & he don't die young -
He'll probably just ride away -

A cowboy loves smoky ole ~~~~ pool rooms &
    mountain mornings -
little ~~~~ warm puppies & children and
    girls of the night -
them that don't know him don't like him
    and them that do sometime don't
    know how to take him -
He ain't wrong just different and his
    pride won't let him do ~~~ things
    to make you think he's right -

The Willie Nelson-Waylon Jennings duet, "Mamas Don't Let Your Babies Grow Up to Be Cowboys," written by Patsy and Ed Bruce, became a Grammy-winning country hit in the late seventies.

Two rare items from one of the greatest songwriters of the seventies: Bruce Springsteen.

10th Ave Freeze Out

Tear drops on the city bad scooter
searchin for his groove
Seems like the whole worlds walkin
pretty and you can't find the room to
move
Well Everybody better move over that's
all
Cause I'm runnin on the bad side
and I got my back to the wall
ready for the
10th Ave Freeze Out

I was stranded in the jungle tryin
to take in all the heat they was
givin
the night is dark but the sidewalks
bright and lined with the light
of the livin
From a tenement window a transistor
blasts!
Turn the corner things got real
quiet real fast I walked into
a 10th Ave
I'm all alone... / kid..... / on your own, you own...
and you can't go home
When that change is made uptown I'm just
gonna sit back easy + laugh / the scooter
and the big man gonna bust this city in
half / when the big man plays it hot even
the heavy hitters shoot their shot when
he plays the 10th Ave

Stayin' Alive

Robin Gibb was interviewed from his home in Florida, with the help of his wife.

At what stage in the writing process of "Stayin' Alive" were you when you started writing ideas on this boarding pass?

The song was written, but the title at that time was "Saturday Night." The new title and the words "Stayin' Alive" fitted into the place of "Saturday Night" in the song, and the old title of "Saturday Night" and the song "Night Fever" gave the title *Saturday Night Fever* to the film, which was originally called *Tribal Rites of a Saturday Night.* We were looking for another two words meaning "to survive": It was a toss-up between "buried alive" in New York City or "stayin' alive" in New York City. We chose the right title.

Had you seen the movie yet when you started working on the song?

We saw nothing of the film until it was out. We had already written the songs for our new studio LP before we were approached about the film. They adapted the film for our music.

When you were working on the song on the plane, were you listening to a rough track on cassette?

No, the song was already written. We just changed the words and wrote them on my boarding pass—I'll write on anything at hand.

How long did it take to write "Stayin' Alive"? What was the usual way you and your brothers would write a song?

"Stayin' Alive" took one night. We'd sit around a cassette recorder and just shoot out ideas. We'd brainstorm two or three hours at a time. This is still the way we write.

(Archive Photos/Fotos Int.)

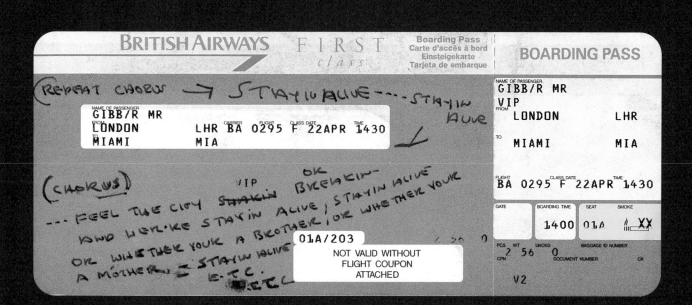

BRITISH AIRWAYS   F I R S T   Boarding Pass   BOARDING PASS
class   Carte d'accès à bord
                     Einsteigekarte
                     Tarjeta de embarque

(REPEAT CHORUS → STAYIN ALIVE ---- STAYIN
                                        ALIVE

NAME OF PASSENGER
GIBB/R MR
FROM
LONDON   LHR CARRIER BA 0295 FLIGHT CLASS DATE 22APR TIME 1430
TO
MIAMI   MIA

(CHORUS)   VIP   OK
--- FEEL THE CITY STAYIN BREAKIN-
KIND WE LIKE STAYIN ALIVE) STAYIN ALIVE
OR WHETHER YOUR A BROTHER, OR WHETHER YOUR
A MOTHER -- STAYIN ALIVE
            E.T.C. ETC

01A/203

NOT VALID WITHOUT
FLIGHT COUPON
ATTACHED

NAME OF PASSENGER
GIBB/R MR
VIP
FROM
LONDON   LHR
TO
MIAMI   MIA

FLIGHT BA 0295 CLASS DATE F 22APR TIME 1430

GATE   BOARDING TIME SEAT   SMOKE
        1400   01A   XX

PCS WT   UNCKD
CPN 2 56 0   BAGGAGE ID NUMBER
                 DOCUMENT NUMBER   CK
V2

On and On

STEPHEN BISHOP

(Lynn Goldsmith)

P ianist and songwriter John Jarvis interviewed Stephen Bishop.

Tell me about what kind of music you heard as a kid.

I was a newspaper boy, planning to become a history teacher, listening to the Limelighters, folk music, when this couple pulled up to a light in a convertible and started to make out. Their radio was pretty loud, and I heard a song that sounded like some kind of magical thing. I just stood there and took in that image with that music. The song on the radio was "I Want to Hold Your Hand," by this new band called the Beatles. I was playing clarinet at the time, but that [song] really turned my head around.

You told me that some people pass you on the street and start singing "On and On." What does that feel like?

It feels like a big-brother kind of thing, or an old pal. I'll be in concert and go into it, and it seems like suddenly people like you more. It's weird. I've been in an elevator and heard some woman who sounds like she's on mescaline come through the speaker with a big orchestra singing "On and On," and I'll look around and everybody will look real serious and I'll feel like laughing.

At the moment you wrote it, did you think there was something special about it?

I have a lot of songs that have stories that go along with them, but "On and On" didn't really have a big, funny story. I was living in Silver Lake in about 1975, and I was walking down to the store and just wrote in a slip of paper in my wallet "On and On," as a title. Then one day I was just looking through the titles in my wallet for ideas, and I saw it in there. I went into my bedroom and sat on the edge of the bed and looked out the window—my landlady had all these pretty flowers—and I guess more than any-

thing I imagined that I was somewhere else. People always ask me if I was in Jamaica when I wrote it; I *wanted* to be in Jamaica. Later on, after it was a hit, I was at a party and Rita Marley, Bob Marley's widow, walked up to me and said, "You wrote that song 'On and On' about Jamaica," and I said, "Yeah, that was me." She said, "You know, Jamaican women, they do not steal your money and break your heart." She got kind of mad, you know.

Actually, on the rough draft it says "feed you mangoes and break your heart."

Yeah, right, "feed you mangoes." I was trying all sorts of things, and thank God I didn't go with some of those lines—because some of them are terrible, you know. "Five- and ten-cent store," "Catch a plane, take a ride into town"—okay, that's just great, Stephen.

"Catch a plane"—why did you reject that? Was it the wrong image, or it didn't sing well, or what?

It was because it was lousy.

Were you just singing nonsense words to find your way into it, or did you already know you wanted a lonesome-Sue-and-Sam and then try to build the lyrics around that?

It's hard to remember, really. I think I always sing mumbo-jumbo lyrics, just whatever comes into my head. I already had the title, so I knew where I wanted to go. Probably back then my lyric style was to throw in that Sinatra reference and to mention different things that everybody would know.

I'm glad that I trimmed it up; some of those lyrics are just horrible. I think that one of the hardest things to do with lyric writing is editing—self-editing. You get real attached to things, and it's so difficult to go back and rewrite them. It's a painful process.

Did Sinatra ever do the song?

No. I always wondered if Sinatra ever heard it! I thought maybe one day I'd open my door and there'd be a brand new shiny bicycle with a big ribbon saying "Love ya—from Frank" or something.

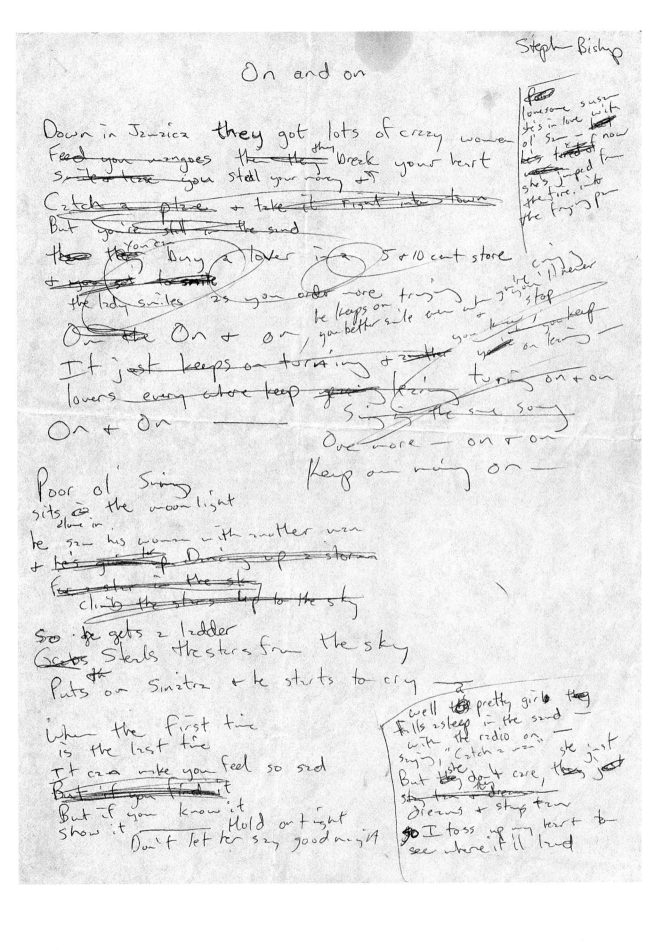

Stephen Bishop

On and on

Down in Jamaica they got lots of crazy women
Feed your mangoes they break your heart
Smile to tease you steal your money and
Catch a plane & take it right into town
But you're still in the sand
You can buy a lover in a 5 & 10 cent store
& you get to smile
the lady smiles as you order more trying crying

On the On & on, you better smile you bet you'll never stop
he keeps on
It just keeps on turning & the you keep you keep
lovers every where keep going trying turn on & on
On & On ___ Sing the same song
Once more — on & on

Keep on going on —

Poor ol' Sinatra
sits in the moonlight alone in
he saw his woman with another man
& he's Dancing up a storm
For a star in the sky
climb the stars up to the sky

So he gets a ladder
Gets Steals the stars from the sky
Puts on Sinatra & he starts to cry

When the first time
is the last time
It can make you feel so sad
But if you know it
But if you know it
show it   Hold on tight
Don't let her say goodnight

well the pretty girls they
Falls asleep in the sand
with the radio on
singing "Catch a ..." she just
But they don't care, they just
start to dream
dreams & stays true
So I toss up my heart to
see where it'll land

PART FOUR

The MTV

Years

My
True
Song

Stephen Bishop

August 4,
82'

Separate Lives

Jay
Gryden
Andrew
Gold

You called me from the phone in your hotel
All full of romance
For someone that you'd met __ ohh __
~ you were sorry ~

TAYLOR

~~You told me~~ Telling me how sorry
you were, leaving so soon.
That you __ miss me sometimes
When you're along in your room
Do you feel lonely too? + Do I feel lonely too

1st
les
eyes
alize
onize
knows
survive
ties
size
music
eyes
sympathize
disguise
compromise
wild byes
goodbyes
cries

I don't
believe
in
compromise

play with
my heart

You have no right
to ask me how I feel   I don't believe
You have no right   in
to speak to me so kind
~~I don't believe in keeping ties~~ ~~sympathize~~ happy to be
I can't go on holding onto this   survive
Now that we're living Seperate Lives

(I don't believe in holding any ties

We were so young
Walking through a dream
We had no right

~~I tried so hard just let you go~~
I held on to letting go,   let you go
~~Maybe~~ ~~held~~ ~~and I tried~~ so hard
+ If you lost your love of mine   If you lost
You never let me know   love for me
    "   "   told me so

50

Lives in the Balance

**JACKSON
BROWNE**

(Henry Diltz)

What was it like growing up with a singer/songwriter for a father?

My dad sang, and he wrote songs, but he wasn't really a singer/songwriter; mainly he played Dixieland piano. He played in speakeasies; he played in Mexico; he used to hire Django Reinhardt to play parties in Germany for *Stars and Stripes* right after the war. There's a picture of him playing with Django at a party, and it's been a family talisman all my life. So by the time I was nine or ten, I was playing trumpet, trying to copy Louis Armstrong and Red Nichols.

You were playing trumpet? Really?

As a matter of fact, if you listen to my singing—I've got a song I'm working on today, and the vocal is trumpet-like. There's no vibrato. It's as straight as possible, as straight as I can make it.

For all this early jazz influence, it's hard to hear a lot of jazz in your music, really.

Well, I call it jazz, but it was Dixieland; and it's actually very close to blues and folk music. Rock 'n' roll comes from jazz and blues and folk music. And country comes from folk music. I always thought that rock 'n' roll was exactly the same thing that folk music had been for the previous couple hundred years. Just because it was on the radio, and had become an industry, didn't mean that it wasn't made the same way—people passing things around and changing them and making them their own.

When did you start writing? What was the first song you wrote?

I was just listening to a demo I made when I was about seventeen, and it wasn't very good. I remember thinking, Well, I can't sing but at least I can write. Now I know I couldn't write either. The first song I wrote was like a Jesse Fuller song. It was a cross between San Francisco Bay

blues and "You're No Good," the song from Dylan's first album; I think it was called "Happy Woman Blues." It was about this woman who was only happy when she was walking all over me or something. I was very influenced by Dylan, but what really changed it for me: I walked into the house one day, and he's sitting at the piano, and he's playing, all by himself, a really, really cool version of "We've Got to Get Out of This Place" by The Animals, with this big octave left hand, and this arpeggio right hand. He was my younger brother.

Tell me how you came around to writing "Lives in the Balance."

In about 1983, while I was touring, I read two books about Vietnam—*Dispatches,* by Michael Herr, and *A Rumor of War* by Philip Caputo. Then I read *Salvador* by Joan Didion, and it really affected me. I'd been reading these books about a war that was over ten years before, that exposed the government's lack of honesty about what they were doing and when and why they were doing it. I'd assumed that was all in the past. And *Salvador* made it clear that the same stuff that had gone wrong ten, fifteen, twenty years before was still going on. I didn't set out to write about it, but the song started coming out of me on a trip to Australia, where I was visiting my son. I remember sitting in this hotel room, and this thing came out. That's the thing about songwriting for me: I don't give myself assignments. Usually I have an idea that develops, germinates over a period of time, and finally just comes out in a song. There's a lot of anger and passion in that song, because you find that it's not enough that so many Americans and Vietnamese died in Vietnam—[the government] looks at it as something they lost, and they want a chance to prove they can win. During the entire period I was writing "Lives in the Balance," I was part of a grassroots movement to get the U.S. out of Nicaragua; obviously, they found another place to do their war, in the Gulf. Still, the real value of a song like this is as a place to focus your ideas and your beliefs, to find out what you know.

I've been waiting for something to happen
For a week or a month or a year
With the blood in the ink & the headlines
And the sound of the crowd in my ear
You could ask what it takes to remember
Cause it's something that's happened before
With a people
Cause you know that we've seen it before
When a people care more for
And a country is drifting to war

I've been waiting for something to happen
For a week or a month or a year
With the blood in the ink & the headlines
And the sound of a crowd in my ear
You could ask what it takes to remember
When you know that it's happened before
When a government lies to the people
And a country is drifting to war

I've been waiting for something to happen
For a week or a month or a year
With the blood in the ink & the headlines
And the sound of the crowd in my ear
You can ask what it takes to remember
When you know that it's happened before
When a government lies to a people
And a country is drifting to war
There's a shadow on the faces
Of the men who the guns
To the people in the places

Fame

IRENE
CARA

Dean Pitchford wrote the lyrics to the Oscar-winning theme from the movie.

This is the kind of rough I like, because it's really messy. It shows that you guys were really working.

In the right corner the logo is drawn. I drew that because it was the first time I had any indication that the title of the movie had been changed. They showed me a mockup using that baseball typeface—without knowing it, you subliminally think New York when you see that. And so I was doodling on the lyric sheet; it was the first time I saw the title rendered the way they wanted it.

Some of the other lines on this sheet . . .

Yeah, some of them really stink. I was grasping at straws! But isn't that the part of the process we all go through the most?

When the script was sent to me, it was called *Hot Lunch.* As a matter of fact, they didn't call it *Fame* until well after the movie was wrapped. The scene the song "Fame" was written for had already been choreographed and shot, but they shot it to a Donna Summer track. Alan Parker decided it was going to be called *Fame.* When Michael Gore [music supervisor for the film] called me and said, "The movie is now called *Fame,* try to make that a song," I was aware of the [David] Bowie "Fame"—tough neighborhood to move into. So then I began to work, and I must have worked for two weeks on the lyric, and Michael kept saying as soon as I had something—anything—going, he'd be able to sit down and write at the piano. And I'd go over there every day and work for three, four, five hours just hammering away at different approaches to the subject of fame. How do you write that without saying, "I want fame, I want glory, I want money"?

Finally, I wrote a lyric that's now history, but from top to bottom it made sense, held together, and he said, "Leave this with me, I think I can write something to this." About 12:30 that night he calls me: "Dean, Dean, I think I've got a chorus for us." So I go over the next day and he plays me what is now the chorus of "Fame." And I immediately recognize that it's fabulous. At the same time, I realize it doesn't fit the lyric I'd just spent two weeks on. So the entire lyric went out the window, and I began all over again.

That hurts.

It hurt, but I began all over with a brand new lyric to the melody—such was my belief in the melody. What happened was, when we had the melody, and he went *{sings tune}* and said, "So there'd be a call-and-response, and she'd sing this part, and then they go 'Fame,' and then she sings—" And I'm standing next to him at the piano, and I say "You mean something like, 'I'm gonna live forever,'" and he says "Ooh, ooh, write that down." And in that moment I came up with that line. It was just the first thing that had occurred to me, and that was when both of us looked at each other and had to agree that the chorus and that line and his melody were far better than anything we'd ever done before, and we should throw out everything else and start with that line and move forward.

Fame
T.M.

A:

Baby, look at me
Ｙou don't ~~really know~~ me
1. [You think I'm someone else] *Good*
Someone not as fine as you are
Someone who will never go far *You aint seen what I've got to give*
~~JUST WAIT!~~

To be the best ~~fuck out~~
You ain't seen the best of me yet

I'll tell you what you see
And tell me what you see

2. ~~You could never know~~ *feel* } *I got more in me*
How much I ~~hide~~ inside *Set it free*
Waiting for the chance to get out
~~Waiting til I can break out~~ *Don't you know who I am??* ○ *Gimme time, I'll make*

I can catch moon in my hand

you ain't seen the best of me *but*
you forget – blah blah

Name – Remember my name *My name will be fame*
~~...~~ name

FAME
I'm gonna live forever
I'm gonna learn how to fly *Show me a stairway to heaven*
HIGH ~~Give me a piece of the sky~~
make me a million *make me a stairway to heaven*
I'm gonna make ~~it~~ to heaven
~~Cut me a piece of the sky~~ *I'm gonna never say die*
People will touch me and cry FAME!
~~WHY~~ *FAME* (People)
Why can't you see I'm a ~~legend~~? *winner* *see*
I'm gonna ~~dance like a flame!~~ *Waiting to get in the game.*
FAME *light up*
I feel things coming together
Then I'll be living forever *I'm gonna live forever*
Then you'll remember my name.

A fame
B?
I feel I think it's (things) coming together

B:

1. You don't really know me
You ain't seen nothing yet
Even though I'm trying to be tough ‖ *Can you shoot me straight up to the top?*
Can't you see I'm falling in love *Take my love – – – – what I got to give*
WITH YOU *– hold me tight*

2. I've got magic in me
I've never let it out *I want you to know.* *Baby I'll be tough –*
Can't you see behind the disguise? *There's magic in my soul* *Those things might*
[Can't you open your eyes? (And see...)] *where get too tough*

★ → *I got what it takes!!*

~~I'm heading for~~ *Remember my name –*
FAME
I'm gonna live forever
I'm gonna learn how to fly
HIGH – I – *feel it coming together*
~~I'm gonna make it to heaven~~
Cut me a piece of the sky *I'm only asking you why.*
WHY
Why don't you see I'm a ~~legend~~? *winner* – *Heaven – going to heaven –*
~~Why can't I play in your game?~~ *travel to heaven*
FAME *make it to heaven*
~~Then I'll be living forever~~ *Then maybe I'll live forever*
Than you'll remember my name.
~~Baby,~~

Dripping is ...
Dripping is Fame

Promises in the Dark

PAT
BENATAR

Tell me a little bit about your early memories of music.

Growing up, all I heard was classical stuff and all those old forties' musicals and Judy Garland, that kind of thing. Frank Sinatra. No contemporary stuff whatsoever. And I studied classical music.

You were going to be an opera singer, but you took a big left turn.

Yeah. Because I was listening to Led Zeppelin and the Stones and trying to sing Puccini, and that didn't make much sense. I sounded like Julie Andrews anytime I tried to sing pop music.

Were you writing back then?

No. You know, I've always done poetry and I've always done stories, but I didn't really write songs. I mean, it never even occurred to me to write songs. I'd always sung other people's music. I spent most of my time emulating everybody—until there's nobody left to emulate, and that's when your own style comes out.

Your early hits had a kind of mystery thing, mostly in the verse, almost a kind of whisper, and then all of a sudden the chorus would kind of explode.

I don't think it was conscious in the beginning, but as the record company realized that this made the money, they thought, okay, you have to do this all the time. That pretty much started the war—the dollar-versus-creativity wars. At first it just came out the way it came out, and then it got very contrived, and that's when it really got uncomfortable, because you're not really evolving. But if you lay the records in a line, you can see when their influence stopped—which was about *Get Nervous*—and then they quit. They weren't allowed to get their fingers in the pie anymore, so the writing changed—for better or worse, you know, because sometimes you'd go

way off because you had nobody holding the reins at all.

You began writing with Neil Geraldo, which must have been strange—to write with your mate.

It was very interesting, because there's so much insight into the other person, and it's really a dance because you have to decide how much you want to reveal. Like what you're feeling about that person, if it's a song pertaining to your relationship. With "Promises in the Dark," I was so—I was embarrassed by it so much because it was really what I was saying about him, and the kinds of things I really didn't want to say that he should know. When I wrote the lyrics, I slid them under the door to his music room. I mean, you know, I was twenty-seven years old. I was still so freaked out about it that I slid it under the door. I couldn't bear it face to face, you know?

On the rough draft, you have little notes all over it—"Armed and Ready," you wrote, and a little flower and "Me and Spi."

Yeah, that's what I call him [Neil]. I call him Spider.

When you guys write, do you ever use any tools—do you always put the tape recorder on?

Oh God, no. For me, the one thing is that it really has to be an organic process. You know, there's lots of writers—and this is no criticism of the way anybody else does it—but I can't sit down and say, "We should go in there and write a song that's up-tempo, and let's sing about this." So there's no dictionaries and I never use a thesaurus. I never use anything like that.

Soul to pen.

Yeah, that's it. It's coming right out or it ain't, and believe me it's agony and it stinks, but you know what? At least when I'm done . . .

(Archive Photos/Fotos Int.)

Promises In The Dark

Never again isn't that what you said
I been through this before ... gone
... This time ... think ... head.   You
No one would ever hurt ~~you~~ me again.
And if there was gonna get done ...
                    where + when   call
                                           2:32

Just when you think ~~it~~ you got it done
Remember now ... to be found
They whisper Promises in The Dark

*Armed + ready
V1 Armed + ready you ...
          you thought love battles in the night
          But this many opponents make you weary
                    of the fight

          They whisper Promises in the Dark...

need ...
B8! Promises you know what they're ... soak ... (coming)

My Bologna

**WEIRD AL
YANKOVIC**

*Y*ou've been doing this for a long time. Did you listen to novelty records as a kid?

Sure. I'm sure you know *Dr. Demento.* That's how I got my start. When I was twelve years old one of my friends turned me on to his show, and I was immediately hooked. People like Spike Jones and Stan Freberg and Tom Lehrer, whom I'd never heard before—people who were popular in the forties and fifties and sixties. I just thought, Wow, this is so cool. So I started writing my own songs, and I sent them in on a cheesy little compact cassette, and he actually started playing some of my stuff on the radio. That rough draft of "My Bologna" I guess I wrote when I was nineteen years old.

Was it really your first one?

It was recorded in the bathroom across the hall from my campus radio station. It literally was. It was me and my accordion, inside the bathroom. We recorded it in the radio station production room and ran the lines across the hall in the bathroom, set the mike up by the urinals, and I did it in there.

So when you write, does it all come very naturally? Do you hear a record once and get the idea, or do you have to work at it?

I guess I wrote more spontaneously back then, because I didn't think, Well, this is going to be on a major-label release. But I was always pretty anal about songwriting. The good ideas would come spontaneously, but then I'd spend a week or two just gathering ideas in a three-ring notebook, and every time I'd get an idea related to that topic, or a joke or a gag, I'd scrawl it down. Then, when I had a dozen pages of random notes, I'd organize them into some kind of cohesive pop song format.

Lorri O'Grady, Weird Al's girlfriend at the time he wrote the song, supplied the original lyric sheet for Songs in the Rough.

How did you first get this rough draft?

The single had come out in December of 1979, and he gave it to me, I'd say sometime around February or March of 1980. He gave me an envelope that had an article about him from his college newspaper, along with a letter and a few other things, and he said, "I'm also enclosing the original lyrics to 'My Bologna.'"

And you looked at it and it said, "My Bologna," and you just said, "This is the kind of thing that . . ."

This is the kind of guy that I want to go out with, yes.

MY BOLOGNA

Ooh my little hungry one
Hungry one
Open up a package of my bologna
Ooh I think the toast is done
The toast is done
Top it with a little of my bologna

CHORUS Never gonna stop
Eat it up
Such a tasty snack
I always eat too much
And throw up
But I'll soon be back for
My my my yi yi woo!
M-m-m-my bologna

Spreadin' on the mustard now
A-show me how
Spread it on some slices of this bologna
Hopin' that we don't run out
A-don't run out
If we do I'm sure that I'll miss bologna
(REPEAT CHORUS)
M-m-m-my bologna
M-m-m-my bologna
(INSTRUMENTAL)

Better add a lettuce leaf
A lettuce leaf
Put it in the sandwich with my bologna
Like it more than ham or beef
A-ham or beef
Though I've never asked myself why bologna

OVER →

We Got the Beat

Charlotte Caffey wrote the Go-Gos' anthem.

"We Got the Beat" was your second or third single, wasn't it?

It was the second single—"Our Lips are Sealed" was the first. It went to number two nationally; Joan Jett's "I Love Rock 'n' Roll" was number one. I remember that particular week—I think the Pretenders had a song, and Joan Jett was number one and we were number two, and I remember being struck by that: "Wow, there's a lot of women in this." It made me feel good.

So you wrote it on guitar?

Actually, it's kind of a funny story. We were considering doing "Going to a Go-Go" as a cover song. We thought, Oh, that would be clever. And I was listening to that song all day, and something clicked in me and I thought maybe we shouldn't do a cover song, maybe I should try writing something. And then at midnight I turned on the TV—*The Twilight Zone,* at midnight, and literally five minutes later, this whole song just came to me. And the thing is, I don't remember which episode of *The Twilight Zone* it was. It was one of those frantic things—the song was in my head faster than it was coming out.

What's different about this rough draft is that you've really outlined the whole vibe of the song for the band. You put all sorts of notes on the side—"bass beat," "J + C + B," then "splash sung in unison."

That was all about the background and the girl-gang kind of chorus thing we wanted to do. I kind of wanted to do something that was danceable, but I wasn't consciously trying. I wrote more Beatle-y stuff, and I was trying to do something a little more straight, with a beat. I really don't know what I was trying for exactly, but that's what came out.

Strong Solid Drum Beat

We got the Beat

1) See the people
walking down the street
fall in line,
just watchin' all their feet

Beleive Adam {

they don't know
where they want to ~~get~~ go.
But they're walking in time, walkin in time

Chorus {
they got the beat, they got the beat
they got the beat

All the kids
Gettin' out of school

G C B unison {

~~Cou't wait till they do~~   they can't wait
so they can all be cool
hangin' around
till Quarter after twelve
s where they fall in line, they fall in line

Chorus {
~~got got~~ Kids got the beat, kids got the
~~got~~
Kids got the beat

refrain (Everyone gonna catch our ~~real~~) ?
~~bust~~
they won't know   what hit them etc.

Go-Go music
really makes us ~~them~~ dance
Do the pony

(right margin, circled, top) G + C + B Spoken then Sung in unison ↑ We got the Beat repeat repeat etc.

(right margin, lower) repeat repeat — we got the Beat

Invisible Touch/Sussudio/One More Night

PHIL COLLINS/ GENESIS

(Archive Photos/Fotos Int.)

I loved the songs on your first solo album. It's odd that you would start that late as a songwriter; usually people start writing at an earlier age.

I was writing bits and pieces. When I was in Genesis, I contributed verses or choruses or bridges or just arranged other people's material. But my interests were not so much in songwriting as in playing. So when my first marriage broke up, at that point, emotionally, I was compelled to start writing my thoughts down, trying to put them to music. Not with a view to making an album, 'cause that was the last thing on my mind. I just was trying to get these emotions out, almost like messages.

What were the early influences on your writing?

The Beatles and Motown. Anything, really, in the sixties, Northern Song–wise, but I mean mainly the Beatles. But that didn't really influence me early—more later, when I started writing. That's when I sort of looked back. I still carry the Beatles' stuff around. That has been my main influence.

When you write, do you incorporate your drums as part of the song? Instead of just writing on piano . . . Some of your songs are so drum-oriented, like "Sussudio."

That particular song, I was trying to force myself into writing something dance-oriented—something I really hadn't managed to do, successfully at least, at that point. So I just set up the right tempo and a machine. Being a drummer who writes songs, I never have a band to play with me when I'm writing. Sometimes the machine's doing a real drummer's job, in which case I'll replace it later. Or sometimes the machine I use will create an atmosphere and be half of the song, so it's hard to take it away—which is why a song like "In the Air Tonight" has the drum machine on it. Lyrically and melodically I tend to write as a drummer, so it's all very rhythm-oriented. "Sussudio" is one word, but because of the rhythm of the song—{sings} da, da, da, da, da . . .

Explain that title. At one point I asked you about it, and you said it's like "Be Bop a Lula."

I remember saying that, but I hadn't thought about it until you just mentioned it. It's a kind of nonsense thing that just sounds nice. But the way I write words I'm sure is the same way you do. You start playing the guitar or whatever, and it all comes at once, or the direction comes at once.

How is it different writing for yourself and for Genesis? Can you always tell which song will be for which entity?

The last ten years we haven't done anything together that was written solo. We keep solo songs for our own albums. Everything we wrote with Genesis for the last three or four records has been just sitting in a room, the three of us, just writing out of thin air.

Did you do that with "Invisible Touch"?

Yeah. *Invisible Touch* was probably the first album we actually did that with. We really just sat down and had nothing written, and wrote it. The song itself was just based on a guitar riff with Mike [Rutherford], which is the chorus with a repeat echo on it. I just started singing, "She seems to have an invisible touch, she seems to have an invisible touch, uh uh uh uh." And that was it. You slave for two days before that when nothing happens, and then that happens.

(C) She seems to have an invisible touch yeah
she takes control and she takes whatever she
                                          wants
She seems to have an invisible touch yeah
it reaches in and grabs right hold of your heart.

(C) she seems to have an invisible touch yeah
she reaches in and grabs right hold of your heart
she seems to have an invisible touch yeah
it takes control and slowly tears you apart.

                 ever
I don't really know her   even from I only know
she's just a girl I met, don't recall never knew her name
but she crawls under your skin, and you're
                                  never the same

know   wants   sees
I can see she gets everything she wants
         &   to your knees
and now it seems I'm falling

I don't even know her, I only know her name
but she crawls under your skin, and you've never
                                  quite the same
                              now I know
she wants everything she see's

and now it seems I'm falling, falling for her.

Sussudio

There's something that's been on my mind all the time Sussudio
she don't even know my name / I think she likes me all the same
Sussudio
ooh

'Ah' if she called me I'd be there
I'd come running anywhere
she's all I need, all my life
I feel so good if I just say the word, Sussudio

I know that
Hope she don't think I'm too young, my love has just begun,
wait Sussudio
Give me a chance, give me a sign, I'll show her anytime

I've got to have her, have her now
got to get closer, but I don't know how
she makes me nervous, it makes me scared
but I feel so good if I just say the word, Sussudio

Solo.

She's all I need, all my life
I feel so good if I just say the word. Sussudio

One more night

3 Verses

Bass notes
D E♭ F B♭

③ Like a river to the sea
I will always come to you

I can't find the words to let you ~~see~~ know the way I feel
I know its only words
you've heard it all before

I want you more

Ⓥ I've been trying ~~but I can't find the~~ so long to let you know
Let you know the way I feel (now) but I know it's only words
so if I stumble or if I fall believe me

I've been sitting here so long trying to think it out
just staring at the phone
and I was thinking should I call what would shall I say
what if
are you (there) alone (you're alone)

I can't see a time you won't be in my life

one more chance

Higher Love

STEVE
WINWOOD

(Archive Photos)

*Y*ou *started off so young as a writer and performer. I was fascinated by the fact that you were only fifteen when you sang "Gimme Some Lovin'." How did you discover music at such an early age?*

Well, I was lucky; my father was a musician, and his grandmother was a musician, and my grandfather on my mother's side was a musician—he played the fiddle and he was a church organist. It's interesting because I'm trying to encourage my children to take up music, which they're doing, but I was never forced into it. There were odd kinds of instruments lying around; one was a banjo mandola, which is like a tenor mandolin but it's a kind of banjo. And then, of course, there was a piano. I also had an uncle who was a bit of a buff and made tape recorders in his spare time. When he was finished with one he gave it to my brother and me, and we used to mess around with this single-track recorder, doing sound-on-sound when we were about eight or nine.

And you seem to have been listening to the blues pretty early. Did you discover Ray Charles at eleven or something?

Yes, actually. It was again through my brother. He had some friends who played in a New Orleans jazz band, Dixieland kind of band, and I went along and asked if I could play piano with them and made friends with them. Some of them were in art college, and they would take me around to backstreet, specialist second-hand record stores to find American imports that were knocking around at that time.

Would you say that you're an on-again, off-again songwriter? Sometimes you just coast for a while, and other times you'll work really hard?

Well, you see, I only ever wrote songs because as a musician and as a band, we needed songs to play. To write a frame-work to jam on is a little different from writing a song per se. That was really the direction I came from. Writing is still something I'm trying to develop; I'm still trying to come to terms with it. It's never something that comes easy, but I don't think it does anyway to people who do it all the time. But it's fascinating, and I do love writing and I get a lot out of it.

So with "Higher Love," there's a mystical, cosmic aspect to the song: "Give me a higher love."

Will [Jennings] likes to call them—and I agree with him—he calls them non-doctrinal hymns. So that's good enough for me! From the professor.

It sounds like you prefer to co-write most of the time.

I do, yes. I like co-writing. I do write lyrics and have written lyrics, but delegation is the art of leadership! No, it's not really that. But I feel my lyrics are more intuitive, whereas the music I probably understand more thoroughly. The music has to be intuitive, too, but I feel I understand the science and intellectual content of music more than I do literature, perhaps. And Will, who as I say is a professor and a scholar, understands the English language, and several others, too.

By this point, you have pretty wide musical tastes.

I think that there's more than one plane. I think I'd have to go to four corners—something like Little Richard to Richard Strauss to George Jones to Celia Cruz. I think there's two kinds of music: good and bad.

- THINK ABOUT IT —
- THERE MUST BE A HIGHER LOVE —
- SOMEWHERE IN THE HEART / DOWN IN YOUR HEART
- OR HIDDEN IN THE STARS ABOVE —

*/ DOWN IN THE
HEART / RIGHT
OR ~~HIDDEN~~ IN
THE STARS
ABOVE

Y
- THINK ABOUT IT —   HAVE
- ~~ONE~~ THERE STILL IS TIME —
- ~~IS~~ IT IN YOUR HEART OR
- ~~IN YOUR HEART OR~~ MINE —
      ~~IS IT IN~~

                    IS
- ~~SEEMS LIKE~~ THERE ~~IS NO GOOD~~ ANYWHERE
-

THINGS LOOK SO ~~BAD~~ EVERYWHERE —
- ~~LOOK AT THE WORLD~~ NOTHING'S FAIR —?
  IN THIS ~~OLD~~ WORLD WHAT IS FAIR.
  ~~BLACK RAIN FALLS ON THE~~
  WE WALK BLIND AND WE TRY TO SEE —
- FALLING BEHIND IN WHAT ~~WE~~ COULD BE —

                              GIVE
- WHERE IS ~~THE~~ A HIGHER LOVE ? / SEND ME
                              THE/A HIGHER
                                    LOVE

GIVE/SEND ME A HIGHER LOVE —
  SEND ME A HIGHER LOVE —
  ~~I'LL~~ WAIT FOR IT —
  ~~HOPE~~ ~~AND IT'S~~ NOT TOO LATE FOR IT —
- UNTIL THEN I'LL SING MY SONG —
- TO CHEER THE NIGHT SO LONG —
GIVE ME
- FOR A / HIGHER LOVE
- FOR A / HIGHER LOVE
-

- TALK ABOUT IT
-
-     I COULD LIGHT THE NIGHT UP WITH MY SOUL ON FIRE
-     I COULD MAKE THE SUN SHINE FROM PURE DESIRE
      ~~LET ME FEEL SOME~~ LOVE COME OVER ME
      ~~LET~~ THAT HIGHER LOVE (INTO ME

Baby Grand

BILLY JOEL

What was the first popular song that really caught your ear when you were growing up?

Trying to think . . . It was probably a Christmas song—"Angels We Have Heard on High." [sings] It wasn't popular music; it was either a folk song or a Christmas song. I like folk music, Commie songs, union songs. Woody Guthrie was a hero. I started writing pop songs when I was about fourteen.

What did your parents think back then? Did they think, Oh, we're so proud, or Uh-oh, he's getting into this rock thing?

No, my dad and mom had already split up, and my mom was pretty loose. We were kind of the gypsy family—we were the bizarre people in the neighborhood. So she was very supportive. My first batch of songs was all these ersatz Beatle tunes. I was copying other composers' styles; when I write, I'm thinking of other artists doing it, not me. I'm writing for all these other people.

Kind of a Brill Building wanna-be?

I guess so. I always admired Carole King, and I think the Beatles did too. I think they looked at Goffin and King as if they were Gilbert and Sullivan. But I never wrote like a Brill Building writer; I never was able to just crank out music. I always wrote about what I wanted to write, what interested me. I always write the music first. It's the backwards way to write—I end up having to cram syllables into melodic phrases. I believe in the Keith Richards style of songwriting. He talks about "vowel movements": Certain sounds are better for certain melody phrases than others. Sculptors say that the sculpture is within the block, and it's your job to find it. There is something going on in there—there is a story line, a character, a thought, a feeling. What does this music make me feel like?

Do you keep little ideas, little things here and there?

I want to be current with myself; I don't keep a whole inventory of songs. There is a spare parts bin, I will admit to that. But I usually use those as connective tissue, not so much as actual melody or actual chorus. There's a song on my last album, "Blonde Over Blue," that has a middle section that originally went [sings] *woh-woh-woh-woh*, just like the middle section of "Uptown Girl." So there are spare parts.

When you sat down to write "Baby Grand," you wrote that with Ray Charles in mind?

Yeah, I wrote it thinking about his voice, thinking about the key. I was told that Ray Charles wanted to record with me, and I thought, My God, this is one of my idols. He was the big guy. If I could sing like anybody, I'd like to sing like Ray Charles. I try to sing like him. He's got a Leslie tone cabinet in his throat, and it's on slow, and there's a couple of tubes that are shot. I wanted to write something bluesy that would be kind of a standard. And I thought, What can Ray and I do as a duet—what do we have in common? So that was my tribute to the piano. What I'm saying in the song is that when everything else deserts you, you still have your axe. And Ray seemed to me to be a man who has had hardships in his life; he's had loss, betrayal, he's had loves and lost them. He's lived. And I thought this was something that he could identify with, even respect.

And did he?

Well, I sent a tape of the song to Ray, and I was on pins and needles, and he called up and said, "Yeah, it's really clever. I like it. Let's do it." He said he hadn't heard a song like that written since the forties. And I thought, Great! But it was very, very intimidating. The guy walks in the room, and it's like the Washington Monument walked in. And I was just this shy kid, trying not to get in the way. We actually started by playing piano together, which was a great way to break the ice. I would play the main chord progression, and he was riffing all around it, 'cause he's got that great blues style. And we just eased into each other as musicians.

On the actual rough draft, it's interesting how you section it off—you've got numbers on all the verses, and you've put "coda" at the end. I haven't seen any other rough drafts that are that musically literate.

Well, you know, even though I don't read the dots [in written music], I love reading the Italian dynamic words—*Allegretto, presto, forte, pianissimo.* If there's one thing I came away with from learning to read music, it was how to speak Italian.

Began

Baby Grand

Late at night, when it's dark and cold
I reach out for some one to hold, Deep and Blue
She ~~comes through~~ ~~sweet and~~ ~~been~~ lonely
she ~~plays true~~ sweet ~~and blue~~, she's the only one who can
My Baby Grand is all I need

In my ~~time~~ I've traveled everywhere
Around this world, she would always be there
Any~~ day~~ Any hour
All s~~ ~~it takes~~ is~~ is the power in my hands
This Baby Grand's been good to me

I've ~~free~~ had friends, but ~~they did not stay~~ they slipped away
I've had fame, but it ~~slipped away~~ 'it doesn't ~~stay~~ stay
I've had fortune, ~~see~~ it passed ~~to dust~~
I've had women, they ~~don't last with just one~~
~~My Baby Grand will stand by me~~ blown
I've made fortunes, ~~spent them~~ fast enough
As for ~~I've had~~ women, they don't last with just one man
~~Like I just~~ but Baby Grand will stand by me

Soul Provider

MICHAEL BOLTON

Where did you come up with the title "Soul Provider"?

That was Andy [Goldmark], in a kind of moment of, "How do you feel about the title 'Soul Provider'?" You know, as a writer, when you come up with a title that makes you think twice about whether you should go with it or not, you start thinking about what other people might think about it, even if from your heart you feel 100 percent about it. I was thinking, "I want to be your soul provider, I want to stay that way for the longest time," and the more I got into that commitment, I started wondering—in this climate, are women going to think I'm suggesting they stay weak and dependent on a man? That was my actual concern. Are they going to misunderstand? Of course, the upside of having a hit is you get to do interviews to express how you feel when you're singing the song. And that was just a wide-open feeling of wanting to be there for somebody, completely, in every possible way. And that's the way it was taken by the fans, I know that.

So when you wrote the song with Andy, did you play guitar or piano? How does that work, generally?

It's varied. I don't really consider myself a keyboard player, but I play and write on keyboards. But when I write at Andy's little studio, he's got his whole setup already for himself, which is basically just keyboards and some machines. I can't remember whether I had my acoustic guitar or not.

When you're writing, where does the germ of the idea come from?

I write with people; I collaborate with people who only like to write if they have a title. They don't even want to get together unless somebody's got a title. And I'm not from that school. I guess just to survive, when my records weren't selling and I was writing for CBS Songs, I got the Brill Building mentality, where you go into a room and don't come out until you deserve to—until you've got an idea or the beginning of a song. I like the fact that I learned how to sit down and just see how you feel and follow it. I think that being able to just sit down and go inside yourself and find something that means something is a great thing. I've learned to write with nothing, from scratch, to write from a title, to write from a painful experience, to write from an inspiring, uplifting experience, from all of the above.

Do you put the tape recorder on? Do you have a rhyming dictionary?

I've got three sizes of rhyming dictionaries: the big one that stays in the house, the medium one in the office, and the one I carry around, which is one of the mini, plastic-covered ones but it still does the job if you're really searching. Working on lyrics to me is always the toughest—trying to come up with words that say what has already been said, in a new way. What will always need to be said in a new way. And you can't always do it. And of course, you'd like to do it all; you'd like to be clever and deep and moving and write a song that will definitely be around for your children and your children's children. The most important thing is the power of the emotion of a song.

Soul Provider.

I stick to the truth
I stick to my guns
believe me when I tell you baby
that we've just begun
ya don't understand the full intent of my plans

I wanna be your soul provider
I wanna stay the way the longest time
I wanna be your soul provider
darlin if ya let me
I'm gonna be surely will

Takes so long   way it used to be
to grateful love they ought and
staring at a vase that use to
hold your flowers
I go weak, I remember the power
if ya holding me

heart look what ya have done to
me without love, don't know what I'm doing
heart ya must have of my side must
have taken all of me "I feel like I'm
who am I foolin   losin' "
Look what I'm losin

The first page of the rough draft of "Soul Provider," in co-writer Andy Goldmark's handwriting.

I Wanna Dance with Somebody

**WHITNEY
HOUSTON**

Shannon Rubicam and George Merrill helped put Whitney Houston on the charts.

Your hits with Whitney got enormous airplay, didn't they?

GM: Yeah. They had enormous record company support in the beginning, and enormous public support.

SR: I think we got lucky. It's kind of hard to get lucky early on and then go funk.

GM: "I Wanna Dance with Somebody" was the first single on the second album. It went to number one in the first week, and I don't know, but I think that was the first time that that had happened at the time. It was extremely exciting for us to be a part of that.

That's really like dipping into the big songwriter dream bucket.

SR: You know, the extra bonus was that we loved the record, and she had such a great voice.

GM: We had heard of Whitney Houston; she was known as Cissy Houston's niece at the time. But nobody had really heard of her. And when the first tape of her singing "How Will I Know" came back, I heard it and it went *{sings}* "How will I knowwww . . ."

SR: And we thought, Dolly Parton!

GM: She sounded just like Dolly, I thought. I thought, Wow, I wonder how this is going to do.

SR: I mean, I had never heard anybody sing quite like that. And especially not on one of our songs. We sent off the demo with my voice, which is very light, kind of high and sweet. Nothing like Whitney's, so our hair blew back on the first listening. We were thrilled.

GM: She actually ended up using some of Shannon's licks on that and on "Somebody to Love Me." You can hear Shannon in there. It's pretty flattering.

So after you'd already had the success of "How Will I Know," were you trying to repeat her formula with the new song, or how did you go about that?

SR: You know what happened, we were aware that they wanted another song for a new album, and at that point we were working on something else of ours, so we sat down—I remember the day we sat down in our old garage studio, where we had our four-track reel-to-reel tape deck. It had cobwebs and everything. We just sat down and wrote that song. It was really easy to write. We probably wrote the whole thing, lyrics and music, in three hours. And then we did this demo in a day over at a friend's studio.

Now, when you write, do you sit down and just say, "We need to write a new song for Whitney"? Do you do research?

SR: Here's what we've always tried to do. We've always tried to get a hold of her and ask what's going on with her, so we can write something pertinent. But the word to us was, she's not interested in that—just write a good song. So that was the research. And then we sat down and tried to write something that would interest her.

GM: In our experience, you can chase your tail trying to get into somebody else's head. Clearing your mind and sitting down and doing what you do best seems to be our best approach to writing.

So on "I Wanna Dance with Somebody," when you were working on it in the garage—how did you come up with the title?

GM: Shannon actually came up with the first verse on that, and I remember Shannon actually came up with a great image for that verse. It really put somebody in a room with that first image, with the clock striking on the hour and the sun beginning to fade.

SR: Yeah, that song was written in sequence, which is not always the case. It was written verse first, then chorus, and there was the hook, and then the next verse. You know, now I wish I could do that again.

Somebody Who Loves Me (Whitney)

W.H. '86

I wanna dance with somebody
I wanna feel the heat with) somebody
~~with~~
yeah I wanna dance with somebody
with somebody who loves me

prince
cleanse
then
when

bonds
sends
lands
mends
nonsense
sense

invents

home
out
now
how
me
let down
fast

less
mess
press

rest
offense
defense

suspense
pretends
amends
contend

the clock ~~says it~~ strikes up the hour
~~the~~ night is chasing it getting on to night
(they) when sun begins to fade away
there's time enough to figure out
how to chase (my blues away) whirl

been in love with different men
and on spin around the town
in the light of day
but at night I can't think too much
had my chance to get around
I've enjoyed
I been with all kinds of men
I've had fun with different men

there's a man I'm thinking of
(but I don't know where he is

I've been ~~cruising with my friends~~
I've been ~~out to every~~ all the spots
a girl ain't the town
I've been ~~over~~ around the town

sooner or later the music ends
and
seems I always feel let down (love always lets me down)
why do I ask
I can no longer ask for less
I won't even think to ask for less
or if hell settle for less
there's must be someone a man

From a Distance

BETTE
MIDLER

"From a Distance" became Julie Gold's big break.

What did you listen to, growing up?

Age four, *My Fair Lady.* Changed my life forever. And 1964, *The Ed Sullivan Show.* The Beatles. And everything changed. The Beatles became like my religion. I don't even own—no offense—but I don't even own a Rolling Stones record. To me, there was only one white band, only one, and it's the Beatles. Every note, every breath, every squeak on the guitar neck, everything.

When did you start writing, and where?

I grew up in the suburbs of Philadelphia, and I have a baby picture at the piano—sitting on the floor at a baby piano, age one. Age two, sitting on a stool at a little babier piano. Started lessons in first grade.

So you started writing when you were what age, basically?

My earliest, earliest songs were outside in the backyard on a plastic guitar. I don't own a guitar, I don't play guitar. I was just strumming, playing a song to the birds and the bees in the backyard. But when I took piano lessons, starting at grade one, whatever age you hear that song and say to yourself, "That's a great song." So I would say in seventh grade, that's when I started writing songs, and by ninth or tenth grade, I have songs that I would still perform, believe it or not. Not many, but a couple.

One of the things that really interested me was that you were working at HBO when you wrote this song. In a way, you epitomize the typical songwriter, working at a regular job, then one day finally getting your break. So how did it come about?

I was a secretary for seven years there, at the New York production facility. They all knew I was a songwriter; they all came to my gigs—they were my friends and sup-

ported me. That draft, on the HBO paper, is really just the first, the roughest. I used to sit at my desk and try to escape every now and then, and you know how it is when you pick up a pen and you go. You can see where I changed some of the lyrics, but when you're trapped at your desk or in your life, not seeing what or who you know you're put on Earth to be, the line "God is watching us" just sort of comes to you. As it did me.

What was the inspiration for this?

I was just about to turn thirty, which is quite an emotional cauldron, isn't it? I had just been on jury duty, which was a really life-changing experience; we had to convict a man. He'd borrowed a gun, stood outside a bar, took a combat pose, and pumped three plugs into the back of a guy who had been harassing him for years. If you'd heard the whole story . . . he tried everything to not have to do that. He tried to get help from the police, from the neighborhood; he tried to talk to this guy who'd been harassing him. He just went crazy. Then he finally did what he thought he had to do. Meanwhile, he had a family, he was supporting children. He was just a very righteous guy who went crazy.

Meanwhile, my brother, who's my best friend, was just about to get married, so that's a very life-changing, self-examination time; and here I was, working as a secretary, living in one dark room, and for my thirtieth birthday my parents sent me the piano that I'd grown up on—my true love, my one friend, my confidant. And I took the day off from work—crisp, winter's day—and from the crystal blue sky the light was shining down on it. The movers brought it into my house and put it where I'd planned, and they say to me, "You can't play it for twenty-four hours, 'cause it's too cold. It's been on the truck too long." Here I am, finally reunited with my true love, and I can't play it. So I polished it and hugged it. My bed was a loft, about nine feet up, and all night long I kept waking up and looking down, and there it was, you know. The next day, I got up, went downstairs, and completed "From a Distance." That's the whole story.

HBO

Julie Gold

From a distance

the wind blows cold & clear -

and there is no acid rain,

from a distance

you can't sense the fear

and you can not see

the pain.

From a distance ―
~~Are the same~~
A People ~~look the same~~ share a ~~hope~~ dream,
and they sing out ―
          hand in hand -
It's a song to hope
It's a song to peace
It's a song to Everyone

Copperline

**JAMES
TAYLOR**

(Henry Diltz)

When you're writing, where does it
usually come from?

It sort of happens, usually, while I'm playing the guitar. And I think that, somehow, language and music come from a
very similar place. They actually sort of
materialize. I don't really know how it
happens.

*Someone told me that there is no
Copperline. Is that true?*

Well, there's no place specifi-
cally called Copperline, no. It
refers to a sort of landscape, a
place that I have in my mind's
eye that does exist, under
another name.

I wrote "Copperline" with
Reynolds Price, the author.
Reynolds was very helpful to
me in organizing it; he and I
had been working on other
lyrics, which had suggested
things to me about this song,
and which I've used. . . . This
business about watching your
daddy dance, watching from the treeline
or the hedgerows at night, the sort of
Faulknerian idea of a remote and formal
father figure breaking down in the moonlight and dancing. That idea came from a
lyric that he and I were working on

before, and he helped me very much in
putting some order to the thing.

*What did he write in the song? How did you
work together?*

It's so difficult to know exactly, to go line
by line and say, "That's his, that's mine,
that's his." It's such a mysterious process
anyway. . . . I had never heard of tomato
wine before, but that was sort of like a
country thing—people used to make fer-
mented spirits out of tomato juice. He
grew up about twelve miles away from
where I grew up in North Carolina. My
father worked for the University of North
Carolina, and we lived out in the country
on the edge of town, which at that time
was not very large. Chapel Hill itself was
kind of an oasis, but the rest of it was
deep, rural South. The musical and lyrical
end of the chorus of "Copperline" just sort
of came. I was warming up backstage in
Los Angeles waiting to go on stage and do
a performance, and I was in a dressing
room playing my guitar and that phrase
came out, and then the rest just easily followed. I'm sure you've had the same experience. You get a certain amount of the
way into the song and it sort of mysteri-
ously spills out, and then you have to go
back and sort of work on the rest of it. I
think there are probably songwriters who
write with a good deal more method than
I have and who are much more orderly
and disciplined about it, and then people
who really get what they're going for and
have an idea of doing something and then
do it. But it's not easy. I can't do it that
way.

*When you sit down and you're writing and
right in the middle of ideas, do you use a little
tape recorder?*

That's right. And I use a notebook, a
three-ring binder so I can shuffle things
around, and I write on one side and then
I write variations on the other, and I can
open up to both pages. I find myself con-
stantly playing word games in my head—
little puzzles in my brain—and sometimes that produces a song.

124

Copperline

Even the old folk never knew
Why they call it like they do
I been wondering since the age of two

Down on Copperline

(the) One time I saw my daddy dance
Snaking his hips and shakin his hands
Brought it back from the war in france

Down onto Copperline
Halfa mile down to Morgan creek
Hercules and the nose shake
Only living for the end of the week

First kiss ever I took
(the) Stole a page from a romance book
Sky opened and the earth shook

Down on Copperline

No doubt I'm overdue
I cant express my gratitude
I was starvin and she gave food

Took a fall from a windy height
(the) Oh boy you better hold on tight
Pray for love enough to last the night
Down on

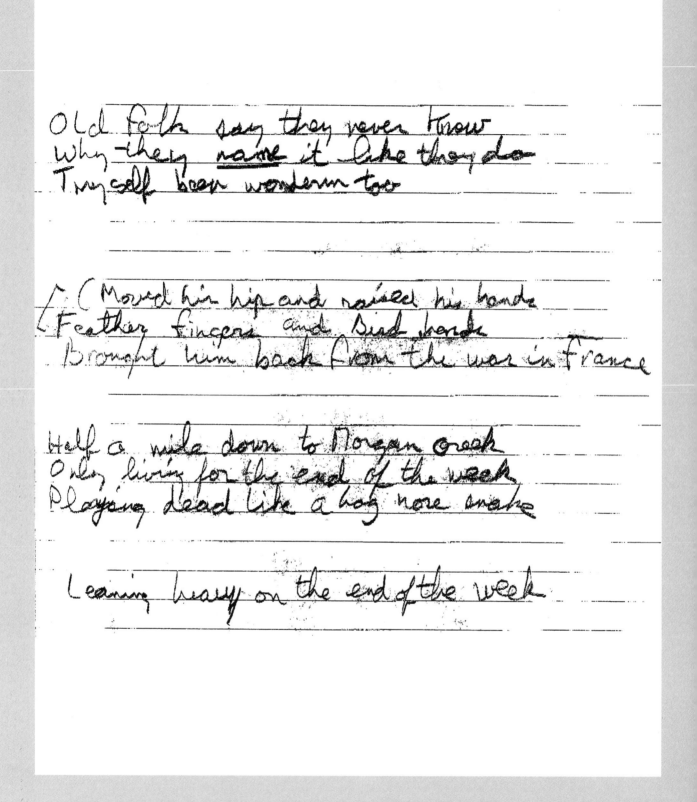

Old folk say they never know
Why they ~~name~~ it like they do
Theyself been wonderin too

(Moved his hip and raised his hands
(Feather fingers and Bird hands
Brought him back from the war in france

Half a mile down to Morgan creek
Only livin for the end of the week
Playing dead like a hog nose snake

Leaning heavy on the end of the week

Worlds apart: James Taylor's southern landscape, "Copperline," and Janet Jackson's "Rhythm Nation."

"RHYTHM NATION"

WITH MUSIC BY OUR SIDE
TO BREAK THE COLOR LINES
LETS WORK TOGETHER
TO IMPROVE **OUR WAY** OF LIFE
JOIN VOICES IN PROTEST
TO SOCIAL INJUSTICE
A GENERATION FULL **OF** COURAGE
~~COME FORTH TO PROGRESS~~ ② COME FORTH WITH ME

PEOPLE OF THE WORLD TODAY
ARE WE LOOKING FOR A BETTER WAY OF LIFE
WE ARE A PART OF THE RHYTHM NATION
PEOPLE OF THE WORLD UNITE
STRENTH IN NUMBERS WE CAN GET IT RIGHT
ONE TIME
WE ARE A PART OF THE RHYTHM NATION

THIS IS THE TEST
NO STRUGGLE NO PROGRESS
LEND A HAND TO HELP
YOUR BROTHER DO HIS BEST
THINGS ARE GETTING WORSE
WE HAVE TO MAKE THEM BETTER

ITS TIME TO GIVE A DAMN
AND WORK TOGETHER COME ON

I Touch Myself

Billy Steinberg co-wrote Divinyls' ode to auto-eroticism.

You wrote "I Touch Myself" with a group, the Divinyls. Isn't that unusual, to write with a group that way? Have you done it very often?

Well, at one point in time, Tom Kelly and I used to write alone together and then go out and seek covers. But we started to realize that if you could get the artist in the room with you, you could write something that would suit them perhaps better than something you might come up with on your own.

It's almost as if you and Tom came from a band. Your writing style is more rock-oriented, not just some songwriter trying to get a Top Forty hit.

I appreciate that, because I've really gone out of my way to try to be sensitive to different artists. For example, if I get into a room with Susannah Hoffs, I know that she likes everything from folk music to the Beatles to the Byrds, and I really try to think along those lines. In my life I've liked everything from Holland-Dozier-Holland music, Motown music, to obscure stuff like Captain Beefheart. I have strong opinions, but I like a lot of different kinds of music. It's been fun being able to wear all these different colored hats. Like when Tom and I got together and wrote "Like a Virgin," we were wearing our Motown hat. That was where it stood musically. Then we wrote a song called "I Drove All Night," which was us trying to really do a tribute to Roy Orbison, in his style.

Right, and then over to "I Touch Myself," which is a giant jump, almost a novelty record.

I wrote the lyrics to that song. Whether it's with Tom or anybody else, I always write the lyrics first. I know a lot of people who like to write the melody and then someone will write a lyric to it, but I always start with a lyric, and that was just a lyric I had in my notebook. For my money, I think the first-verse lyric is really one of the best I've ever written.

What was the writing process like?

I got together with Chrissy Amphlett of Divinyls first and we sat in the Cat and Fiddle with a notebook full of my lyric ideas, and the one she liked most was "I Touch Myself."

Did she laugh?

No, she thought it was cool. You know, she didn't think it was funny. It just appealed to her. And so we got together the next day, and I put the lyric in front of Tom and he started banging out the chords and melodies, and of course Mark Macenty, the guitar player in Divinyls, who's a great guitarist, came in with some good chords, and then Chrissy would sing sections and make them her own. And that's sort of how it happened.

Writing lyrics can be awfully hard work. Do you find it comes easy for you?

I would never say it comes easy, but if I'm able to write a lyric, I just write it. On a couple of occasions I've been asked to put lyrics to existing melodies, and for me it's agonizing. I started by writing poetry in high school, and I was singing in a rock band, but I didn't play an instrument and I never tried writing a song. Then I started to learn guitar, and it was just a natural progression for me to start trying to sing these poems I was writing.

But songs meant so much to me as a child. Those 45s meant so much to me. My earliest favorites were things like "(All I Have to Do Is) Dream" by the Everly Brothers, "Little Star" by the Elegants, or "Poor Little Fool" by Rick Nelson. Then the Beatles came out and that intensified everything; I must have listened to *Meet the Beatles* eighteen million times, and I also love the excitement in the singles, like "She Loves You" and "Please Please Me." I just went bananas. I can't tell you, I'd hear them and I'd be crawling out of my skin with just the pleasure of those two-and-a-half-minute records.

I aint ashamed
to admit it
But if I had you
to touch me
Baby I'd quit it

The times that we've touched have
all been mirrors I want to see things clearer
+ I've touched myself
I spill myself + then I still myself
you have the key to my (wound) skeleton

I close my eyes I see your eyes

I touch myself (when)
I want you to touch me
I don't want no one else
so   I touch myself

I touch myself
I want to touch you

First There's the wanting
    before
Then There's the having
I'm consumed in/by desire

I close my eyes I light a candle
I fantasize every angle
I see you darlin

When night comes oh darlin
well
I go

I just/want you (I) don't want nobody no one else
when I think about you   I touch myself

It's been such a long time
But I touch myself + wish your hand was mine .

A) I love myself
want you to love me
I search myself
when I want you to find me
I forget myself
    lose
I want you to remind me
I hurt myself
I want you to heal me
I touch myself
I want you to feel me

when I feel down
B) don't want no one
else   I want you
    to hold me

when night comes
alone in my room

I want to remember
how good it feels

how it feels
to be incident
To have pleasure
I know

when you're on me

Baby   my
nerves are't
made of steel

Yvette in English

DAVID CROSBY

You have so much knowledge of harmony. Did you take choir in school?

Yeah, I did, but I didn't study or anything. It mostly comes from the music around the house. My mom played a lot—a ton—of classical music. And that was clear back in the 78s era. Then, when the first LPs came out, the ten-inch LPs, we got a player and my mom had Josh White, Odetta, and the Weavers. But what I really remember was "Dream" by the Everlys. That was the first thing that came across the radio and fucking floored me.

When you sit down to write songs now, how is it different now from the way you wrote back in the sixties?

Oh, it's a lot different now, man. For one thing, I can't legislate writing. I can't say, "Okay, I'm going to sit down and write." It doesn't work.

Do you write from a title?

No—I mean, I might. I write from whatever the fuck—sometimes it's the music, sometimes it's the words, sometimes it's both at the same time, sometimes it's just a scrap and sometimes it's the whole thing and it's like automatic writing and obviously some other part of me has been considering it for a while because it all comes out in one blurb and I haven't ever thought any of those things before, consciously. But some part of me has, because I just write it down.

Do you write lyrics out first and then work on the melody?

It happens every which way. But lately I've noticed a couple of things. One is, very often it happens right when my verbal-crystallization level is falling asleep—the imaginative level of the mind to make those longer jumps, you know? Get a hold of the steering wheel for a second, before you cack, you know. I don't understand how that works, but that's when stuff jumps out of me that I didn't plan on at all. An author friend of mine, William Gibson—he wrote *Neuromancer*—said, "Yeah, that happens all the time, we call it the elves taking over the workshop. That's why all writers have a pad of paper by their bed." The other major change lately has been working on the computer on the lyrics, which makes me a much better editor, because you can cut and paste and cut and paste. You can edit yourself, try different editings of a song, stack them up next to each other, and see how they feel.

But there's no rough draft. That's the problem.

Yeah, there is. I almost always write it out handwritten at first, then I enter it into the computer. I don't write on the computer, just work on it there.

We're using "Yvette in English" here.

Well, "Yvette in English" is pretty good. What I did was I faxed her [Joni Mitchell] a set of lyrics that I wrote in Japan, and then she just ran with it.

You guys didn't just sit in a room and trade ideas: "How about this? How about that?"

No. She was pretty excited. She called me up two and three times an hour to say "How about this" and "How about that," and I would say, "That's fucking wonderful." I've always loved co-writing. I've done it with tons of people, man, and I love doing it. Everybody else is very defensive about it because they're looking to have the publishing and they're looking to make all the money, and I don't fucking care. I love writing the songs.

There's also a social side to it, too—you go over, have dinner, hang out. . . . Do you have songs that you start and get excited about and then decide to finish it the next day—and then the next day you're not as excited about it?

Well, yeah. I have lots of them, but they're in my book or in my computer. I have lots of unfinished ones in my book, and lots of scraps. What Joni told me was, if you have two words in a row that you like, write them down.

(Henry Diltz)

Yvette in English

JONI MITCHELL

Your earlier style of writing was very different from what you're writing now.

Right. That's because I was playing in coffeehouses, and most of the music that I was exposed to regularly was folk music. Although I was a folk musician between 1963 and 1965, by the time I began to write my own music I was no longer a folk musician. I had been exposed to a lot of classical music in my early childhood because I had a hard time finding kids I could play with, and I ended up playing with two classical-music prodigies. They were the most creative kids in my environment. One went on to become an opera singer and one was a child prodigy piano and organ player. Frankie, Peter, and I used to put on circuses annually and raise money for the Red Cross, of all things. We did it of our own volition; they were creative kids and didn't get into role playing [the way other] girls played house and the boys played Roy Rogers and war. I was always the German and had to die in the first act, or else I was Dale Evans and had to stay home and cook. It was hard to find kids that played genderless, creative games, but these boys did.

Sounds like an unusual childhood.

Well, you know, it was a small town, and creativity was odd in the context. It was an athletic town, although a lot of Europeans settled in the community, so there was also classical education afforded. But as far as the thought that you wanted to create music—because I did—I started having dreams at about eight that I could play the piano beautifully and compose music, and I started hearing melodies in my head. So I went to study piano, but the teacher rapped my knuckles; if you played by ear, they slapped you with a ruler. That killed my love of the piano. When I said, "I want to compose music," she said, "Oh, why would you want to compose music when you can have the masters under your fingertips?"

But outside of the classical, what popular music did you hear?

The swing beat stuff. My dad had Harry James records; he was a trumpet player. When I was eleven, we used to listen to Louis Jordan, "Saturday Night Fish Fry." We had a neighbor who was a disk jockey in Edmonton, and he cleared out all his oldies and gave a bunch to me, so I inherited Louis Jordan among them. That was pre–rock 'n' roll, somewhere between boogie-woogie and R&B. So when rock 'n' roll came along, although they said it was a new concept, I thought, It's not that new. It's a tributary of boogie if there's a piano player, and rhythm-and-blues, of course, if there's a guitar player. Rock 'n' roll still had the swing beat to it, which I really loved, you know—the shuffle.

I don't think many people know about this side of you.

When I was twelve, rock 'n' roll appeared in the city. There was a jukebox at the Avenue H swimming pool, and another one at the C M Lunch on the west side. So I took to going to the side of town which would be like going to the Chicano side of town, and from twelve to sixteen I became a rock 'n' roll dancer in the juke joints. I was born in the swing era and loved to dance, always. Then I had polio when I was nine, so my legs were taken away from me for a couple of years. So when my strength came back, the celebration of having legs that moved one in front of the other was not enough. You had to really celebrate. I appreciated having feet that moved.

What's your writing process like now?

I do a lot of writing and a lot of rewriting. A lot of times I have many, many ideas and I have to condense it. Sometimes I write six or eight verses and condense it down to three, depending on the topic.

"Yvette in English," didn't the title of that come first?

No, "Yvette in English" came from some scribblings of [David] Crosby's on a piece of paper. A man meets a French girl, you know, in a Parisian cafe, and nothing much happens. She offers him some bliss. The woman is unnamed.

So he's an old friend, but what made you decide to write with him? You don't generally write with other people.

The only reason I did it with Crosby was because he was making his record and he wanted me to produce him. I didn't want to produce him. He wanted me to co-write with him, but I didn't have any ideas. Did I have any songs I hadn't recorded? No, I didn't. So then he said, "If I fax you this, will you look at it?" So I looked at it, and there were some good lines in it, but it needed structure, rhymes, you know. There was just a premise and a little bit of language. The amazing thing was, with the little bit of stimulation he gave, that thing was done in a couple of days. The music comes easy. It's the words that are hard. So I took what he had and I paraphrased it a lot. He had, "The moon spilt like wine," and I wrote, "Burgundy nocturne tips and spills and they trot along nicely in the spreading stain." He had, "She offers him a little bit of instant bliss," which became a piece of the chorus, and then I gave her a name—Yvette.

A young Joni Mitchell, in the back seat of a car, works on the lyrics of her song "Willie."

(1)

The river m...

we are speaking in tongues you and I
sometimes I can catch how the world
looks through your eyes
~~to~~ and I think Picasso drew you
I wonder what mind blew you
and your leaf-like life my way today
the cigarette burns your finger and
you return to earth
flustered and not sure of your worth
you slide sideways as ~~~~ sleek as a cat
and ~~I slide~~ ~~in my mind~~ ~~I will always remember~~ you moving
like that
The night has ~~come creeping~~ oozed into ~~the~~ electric
cafés and ~~is~~ shadows are stealing all the people
away. Its like an exhibition where all the
pictures are all sold
The walls are getting lovely and I
am getting cold.

A   We're speaking in different
     tongues ~ You~I
A   Sometimes I catch how it
     is in your eyes
     There's no insulation
B   We're wires layed bare
     As we ~~catch~~ fluster along
B   Feeling touched and scared
C   You ~~say~~ in English " Here ~ try some of
     this
C   It's a little bit of instant bliss."

A   It's a cold fatigue ~ the old uphill

A   As the burgundy nocturn tips & spill

B   As we slip along in the spreading
     stain
B   How did I wind up here again
C   You say in English " Here try some of this
C   It's a little bit of instant bliss."

     Your cigarette burns your fingertips
     It falls like firework
     And you step on it
     What blew your beof

...and Joni Mitchell's rewritten version.

Study War No More

WILLIE DIXON

Stephen Bishop spoke with Marie Dixon, widow of the great bluesman, Willie Dixon.

I loved Willie Dixon's autobiography, I Am the Blues. *What a human being. It sounds like he had a lot of fun in his life. What was he doing in the blues?*

Well, the blues was fun to him as well as a business. He enjoyed telling people about everyday life—his songs are about somebody's life today, and it was fun for him to write the lyrics and put them out there and let people hear about it.

Where did he get his ideas for songs? His inspiration?

From old clichés. People would say, "You can't judge the book by looking at the cover" or "Don't judge anyone until you know the person." I mean, most of my race of people use that, but I don't know whether other races say such things. These were just old sayings. Willie heard these words many times, and from that point he wrote songs from them. He added his own words to the sayings.

How did the actual writing happen? How did he work out the music?

He wrote according to what was happening around him. Sometimes he used a piano, and sometimes he used guitar players to help him put the music to it.

It just came to him, then?

Let me give you an example of a song he wrote: "The Same Thing." He and I were sitting in the living room one day, and he said to me, "What would make a good song?" and I said, "I don't know, anything would make a good song, I guess, if you could put words where they would rhyme." And he said, "Well, let's think about a minister. What makes a man go

crazy—when a woman wears her dress so short and tight?" And he started from that, and it was "The Same Thing": "What makes a bulldog fight all night"—he just added his own impression to what makes men so crazy. Another one he wrote was "It Don't Make Sense if You Can't Make Peace." He got this idea from all the wars and all the troubles in foreign countries. Every time you turned on the TV there was something going on, and he said, "This don't make sense. If the world spent as much money trying to make peace as they do making war . . ."

Was this when he wrote "Study War No More"? It seems like the same theme.

No, "Study War" was one of the last things he wrote. In that particular song I think he's telling you about the children, how they need so much. And it's about life. Willie wrote from what he heard. He was a very peaceful man, he was a man who loved peace, he was a man who loved people. And he always tried to write his songs around things that would make ease. Mostly happy—I don't think he ever wrote what people call sad blues.

We're thrilled to have this as Willie Dixon's representation in the book.

That would be one of the greatest things that Willie could hear you say. "Study War" is one that never got publicized—he didn't live to publicize it, you know—but he did want that particular version of that song out there for the younger generation.

How did he feel when he heard all the British-invasion groups, like the Stones and Led Zeppelin, doing his music?

He was happy to see that happen, but he always said that blues was the root of all American music. That was his theory. And he said that from the blues you could take the same music and do it in a rock form. So he was very happy about that.

Study War No More

Ant gonna study. study war no more
" " " " " " " " " "
" " " " " " " " " "
We giving it up. We gonna let it go
" " " " " " " " " " .

1 Won't that be one mighty Day.
When we hear all leaders say.
Would you don't need to cry no more,
We giving it up. We gonna. let it go.

2 Think how stupid. We have bin.
Killing families, of women and men
With all the suffering and hurting to
We gonna make it easy on you — Ant gonna st—

3 Hey Ant we lucky. to still be around,
When so many other have all gone down,
With Different plays and Kind of Deseas.
We hope its time for us to live in love
Think of all the things we done.
Murdering each other with all Kind of Bombs
Now with the Adoms. No one Can live.
Stop taking lives. its time to give —
Ant gonna Study

Song Credits